IT'S ALL IN YOUR HEAD

A Guide
To Understanding Your Brain
And Boosting Your Brain Power

IT'S ALL IN YOUR HEAD

A Guide To Understanding Your Brain And Boosting Your Brain Power

Susan L. Barrett

Edited by Pamela Espeland
Illustrations by Jackie Urbanovic

Free Spirit
PUBLISHING

Dedicated to Scott

Library of Congress Cataloging-in-Publication Data

Barrett, Susan L. (Susan Laura), 1957-
  It's all in your head.

  Bibliography: p.
  Includes index.
  Summary: Discusses the physiology and evolution of
the brain, definitions and measuring of intelligence,
problem solving, and other related topics. Also includes
suggestions for further reading and activities for
stimulating creative thinking and other intellectual
abilities.
  1. Brain--Juvenile literature. 2. Intellect-
Juvenile literature [1. Brain. 2. Intellect]
I. Espeland, Pamela, 1951-   II. Urbanovic,
Jackie, ill.   III. Title.
QP376.B36 1985 153 85-80631
ISBN 0-915793-03-2 (pbk.)

Cover and book design by Nancy MacLean and
Michael Tuminelly

10 9 8 7 6 5 4 3 2 1

Free Spirit Publishing Co.
4904 Zenith Ave. So.
Minneapolis, MN 55410

"The Brain — is wider than the Sky —
For — put them side by side —
The one the other will contain
with ease — and You — beside."

— Emily Dickinson

CONTENTS

INTRODUCTION

Your brain has been custom-made for you.

It's an original. One of a kind. And it came fully equipped with everything you'll ever need (and then some!).

But one thing it *didn't* come with is an instruction manual. So it's up to you to figure out how to use your brain, how to make the most of it, and how to get it to do what you want it to do.

Does that sound like a tall order? It is! Especially since your brain has unlimited potential. What that means is . . . there's no end to what you and your brain can do.

This book is for kids like you who are interested in exploring the possibilities — and capabilities — of their brains.

Maybe you've already noticed that there are lots of books and magazine articles about the scientific features of the brain. The fact is, you could spend eight hours a day for the rest of your life reading about the brain, and you still wouldn't get to everything written about *one single year's* worth of research and findings.

So it's no surprise that this book won't tell you everything about the brain. No book could ever do that. But it *will* tell you some things you want to know.

How do *we* know what *you* want to know? Because we interviewed more than 450 kids ages 8-16 from all over the United States.

What we learned was that most kids were interested in investigating the mysteries of the mind — the "unknowns." Here are some of the questions they wanted answers to:

★ **Why do we dream, and what happens when we dream?**

★ **What is hypnosis, and how does it work?**

★ **What is "déjà vu" all about?**

★ **Can people really bend and/or move objects with their minds?**

★ **What is ESP, and how can we develop it?**

★ **Is it true that people have a "sixth sense"?**

★ **Is it possible to increase or extend the powers of the mind?**

★ **What is intuition, and how can we use it?**

A good way to approach these topics is by first examining some of the facts about the brain — the "knowns." Here are other questions kids thought were worth exploring:

★ **Why are some people more intelligent than others?**

★ **What does an I.Q. test test?**

★ **How did the brain evolve?**

★ **What goes on inside the brain?**

★ **How do we learn and remember things?**

★ **How do right-brain functions differ from left-brain functions?**

★ **What is creativity?**

★ **Is it possible to become *more* intelligent and/or *more* creative?**

★ **How does the brain store memories?**

★ **Are people born intelligent, or is intelligence something you have to work at?**

Have *you* ever wondered about these same questions? If so, you've come to the right place. (If not . . . ????) Maybe you've wondered about other questions. (Maybe someday you'll write your own book).

THE BRAIN HAS MORE ANSWERS THAN YOU HAVE QUESTIONS.

The only limitations on your brain are the ones *you* put on it. Your brain may only be a thousand cubic centimeters in volume — about the size of a grapefruit — but it packs a LOT of power!

We hope you'll use this power to discover *your* true talents and abilities. You may even find some you didn't know you had.

"Do what you can with what you have where you are."

— **Theodore Roosevelt** (*26th President of the United States, author of 17 books, Rough Rider, big-game hunter — and the person the Teddy Bear was named after*)

BRAIN VS. MIND

In this book, we talk about both the "brain" and the "mind." They're not necessarily the same, although the two terms are often used interchangeably. If you want to get picky, here are the definitions:

○ The *brain* is "the part of the vertebrate nervous system that is the organ of thought and nervous coordination, is made up of nerve cells and their fibers, and is enclosed in the skull."

In other words: it's that lump of stuff inside your head that thinks and coordinates all of your bodily functions. It's a *thing* that can be weighed and measured and looked at and studied.

○ The *mind* is "the part of an individual that feels, perceives, thinks, wills, and especially reasons."

If that sounds a bit looser than the definition of the brain, it is. It's generally believed that the mind resides in the brain. But the brain isn't the same as the mind — not exactly.

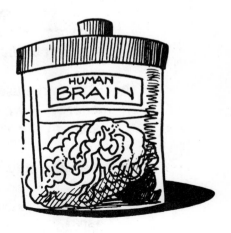

What's the difference? Well, the brain is an organ, a part of the body; the mind isn't. A scientist can put a brain in a jar — but nobody can put a *mind* in a jar.

Definitions of *brain* and *mind* reprinted by permission. From the Merriam-Webster Dictionary © 1974 by Merriam-Webster Inc., publisher of the Merriam-Webster® Dictionaries.

BRAIN STATS

► Each and every second of your life, several billion bits of information pass through your brain.

► Messages within your brain travel through trillions of neural connections at speeds up to 250 miles per hour.

► Your brain generates 25 watts of power while you're awake — enough to illuminate a lightbulb.

► Your brain uses 20% of your body's energy — while accounting for only 2% of your body's weight.

► You use only 1%, 2%, 5%, 10%, or 20% of your brain's capacity (depending on which scientist you talk to!).

WHY BABIES HAVE BIG HEADS

If you have a little sister or brother (or niece or nephew or cousin or neighbor), then you've probably held a newborn baby in your arms.

Maybe you were lucky, and the baby was asleep *and* dry, and you had time to look it over. What you saw was: two skinny arms, two skinny legs, lots of tiny fingers and toes, a cute little tummy — and a *big fat head* (probably bald).

In fact, most babies' heads account for 1/4 of their total length. If that ratio stayed the same throughout a person's life, then a man 6' tall would have a head 1 1/2 feet long!

Why are babies' heads so big? The answer is simple: Because their brains are so highly developed. When a baby first enters the world, its brain is already one-fourth its adult weight. (Even though its body may be only 1/20 its adult weight, give or take a few pounds.)

A baby's brain grows at an amazing rate — one milligram a minute!

■ A 6-month-old's brain is already 1/2 its adult weight.

■ A 2-and-a-half-year-old's brain is already 3/4 its adult weight.

■ A 5-year-old's brain is already 9/10 its adult weight.

For a long time, scientists have been saying that a baby's environment plays an important role in learning. These figures give one good reason why: It's during infancy that the brain grows the fastest and the most.

Babies experience things from the moment they're born (and even earlier). Shapes, lights, colors, sounds, textures, smells, tastes, touches ... and all of these experiences affect the brain in some way.

During the early 1970s, Mark Rosenzweig and his associates conducted a study that proved how important environment is to brain growth and learning.

They raised two groups of rats in very different ways. They put the first group in an "enriched" environment — a big, comfy cage with toys to play with, trapezes and ladders to play on, a variety of foods to eat, daily exercise, and lots of other rats for company. They put the second group in small, empty cages and kept each rat isolated from the others.

The first group was able to learn tasks — like running through a maze — far more quickly than the second group. Later, when the scientists studied their brains, they found that the rats in the first group had grown heavier and thicker *cerebrums* than those in the second group. (We'll talk about cerebrums in a minute; for now, you should know that the cerebrum is the "thinking part" of the brain.)

So the bottom line seems to be that environment has a definite effect on learning and brain development. More about this later. (If you can't wait, see "Nature vs. Nurture," page 43.)

If you want to know more about how environment affects brain development and learning, read:
*** *The Brain Book* by Peter Russell (New York: E.P. Dutton, Inc., 1979), chapter 2.
*** *Growing Up Gifted* by Dr. Barbara Clark (Columbus, OH: Charles E. Merrill Publishing Co., 1983), chapter 2.

Throughout this book, we'll be referring you to other resources — places to go to find out more. One star (*) means an easy-to-read book. Two stars (**) means a not-so-easy to read book. Three stars (***) means a book that's hard to read but worth the effort.

HOW THE BRAIN EVOLVED & WHAT THE DIFFERENT PARTS DO

Millions of years ago, the brain was just a clump of cells called *ganglia*. It was barely a brain at all, and it wasn't very sophisticated. The problem was, it had to get more sophisticated if the life forms that existed back then were going to survive, evolve, and adapt to their changing environment.

Lucky for us, it did. As various life forms moved from water-breathers to air-breathers, from swimmers to crawlers (and some to flyers), their brains grew better and better.

If you want to know more about how the brain evolved, read:
* *Exploring the Brain* by Alvin and Virginia B. Silverstein (Englewood Cliffs, New Jersey: Prentice-Hall, Inc., 1973).
** *The Enchanted Loom: Mind in the Universe* by Robert Jastrow (New York: Simon and Schuster, 1981).
*** *The Dragons of Eden* by Carl Sagan (New York: Ballantine Books, 1977).

Today we actually have three brains in one. Each is a sort of "control center" and has its own jobs to do. Let's explore these "control centers" and find out why they're so important.

The Brain Stem

The brain stem is the oldest and most primitive part of the brain. It evolved more than 500 million years ago — before mammals. It's sometimes called by other names: the "reptilian brain," the "R complex," the "lower brain," or the "hind brain."

The brain stem is really an extension of the spinal cord. The swelling on it is called the *medulla oblongata*. The medulla oblongata regulates your life-support systems — things your body does without thinking. Your heart is beating, you're breathing, your blood is circulating, and your stomach is digesting the last meal you ate because your medulla oblongata is at work.

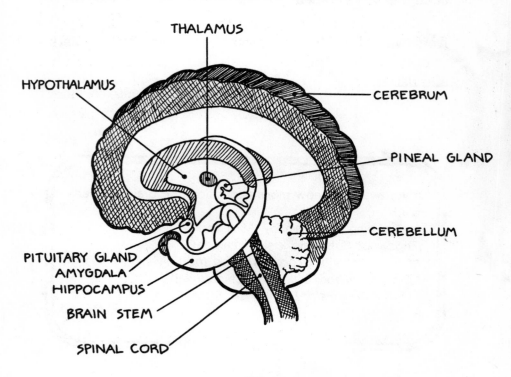

The *limbic system* evolved around 250 million years ago. It surrounds the brain stem like a donut. It used to be called the "smell brain" because of its direct connections to smell and taste receptors. Now we know that it also performs many other functions, including memory storage.

The so-called "mood-altering" drugs affect the limbic system, which is why the not-too-smart people who take them feel emotionally "high" or "low."

The limbic system is made up of the *thalamus*, the *hypothalamus*, the *pituitary gland*, the *pineal gland*, the *amygdala*, and the *hippocampus*.

◆ Your *thalamus* monitors and sorts out messages from your senses so you don't get confused.

◆ Your *hypothalamus* houses your emotions and regulates your body temperature. (Without it, we'd be "cold-blooded" like reptiles.) It lets you know when you're hungry or thirsty, controls your blood pressure, and is the source of your sexual feelings.

◆ Your *pituitary gland* controls the release of hormones which enable your body to produce energy out of the food you eat.

◆ Your *pineal gland* is responsible for the rate at which your body grows and matures. It's like a "biological clock" that's activated by light.

◆ Your *amygdala* can trigger either angry aggression or docility, depending on the situation you're in and which part is affected.

◆ Your *hippocampus* forms and stores new memories.

Another system is located at the upper part of the brain stem. Called the RAS, or *reticular activating system*, it acts like a "master switch" or "alarm bell," alerting your brain to information coming in from the senses. Without it, you'd be in a coma.

The RAS, which is about the size of your little finger, also acts like a "sieve," allowing certain messages to pass through to the thinking part of your brain faster than others. For example, if you were in a house that caught fire, your RAS would react to that information more quickly than to the sound of your neighbor's lawnmower starting up. Somehow it knows the difference between what's important and what's trivial.

Your RAS is useful in still another way: it helps "filter out" sensory stimuli so you can concentrate. Imagine that you're trying to read a book in a busy shopping mall. Your RAS will filter out the crowd noises — but if someone calls your name, you'll hear it.

Tennis pros like Boris Becker and John McEnroe develop control over their RAS. When they're standing on the court at Wimbledon, focusing on the serve that's coming at them like lightning, they *have* to be able to shut out everything else around them. The RAS comes to the rescue!

The Cerebellum

The two-layered "bulge" which sticks out of the brain stem is called the *cerebellum*, or "mini-brain." The cerebellum coordinates your muscles so you aren't a total klutz.

Posture, movement, and the sense of balance are all housed in the cerebellum. We can thank it for making it possible for us to bounce, throw, and catch balls. Plus some researchers think that it may have something to do with emotional development.

When you run a race or practice the piano, it's your cerebellum that shifts your muscles into automatic pilot. The more you practice, the better it gets.

The Cerebrum

The *cerebrum* is the newest and largest of our three "brains." It's also called the "forebrain," the "upper brain," and (for obvious reasons) the "new brain."

The way it evolved is especially interesting. Millions of years ago, this part of the brain was nothing but a "sight and smell" machine that helped animals to locate food and escape from their enemies. In amphibians, it gradually grew a surface layer called the *cortex* (which means "outer rind" — like the rind of an orange).

As animals got smarter, the cortex got larger and became the *neocortex* (or "new cortex"). But the skull didn't grow as quickly, so the neocortex had to find a way to "fit" inside it. It did this by crumpling into wrinkles and folds called *convolutions*.

Your cerebrum is full of convolutions. In fact, if you pulled it out of your head and spread it flat, it would be about as large as the Sunday comics. Your cortex covers your whole cerebrum and is about as thick as a tongue depressor.

What does your cerebrum do? Plenty. You could call it your "thinking cap." Because of it you're able to reason and solve problems. It houses your intellect, your memory, your language skills, and your ability to understand symbols (including numbers and the letters of the alphabet). Plus it makes decisions — after first comparing the new information it receives with information that's already stored inside your head.

Your cerebrum makes up about 85% of your brain's total mass and is divided into two halves, or *hemispheres*. Each hemisphere contains different networks of cells that receive, store, and retrieve information. When people refer to the "left brain" and the "right brain," what they mean is the two hemispheres of the cerebrum.

There's been a lot of talk in recent years about "left brain" and "right brain" functions. We'll get around to that topic later. (If you can't wait, turn to page 49.)

If you want to know more about the inner workings of your brain, read:
* *The Amazing Brain* by Robert Ornstein and Richard F. Thompson (Boston: Houghton-Mifflin Company, 1984), Part I.
*** *The Brain* by Richard M. Restak, M.D. (New York: Bantam Books, Inc., 1984).

"We don't know one millionth of one percent about anything."

—**Thomas Edison** (*inventor of the electric lightbulb and the phonograph and holder of over 1,000 patents — and he attended school for only three months*)

A LOOK INSIDE
YOUR BRAIN

On the surface, most human brains look pretty much the same: light-pink-and-grayish-white, wrinkled, and squishy. Brains can vary in size and weight, but the average male brain weighs 49 ounces and the average female brain weighs 44 ounces.

Some people have smaller brains while others have real whoppers. But brain weight and size have *nothing to do with intelligence*. In fact, "small-brained" people may actually be far more intelligent than "big-brained" people. (Einstein's brain wasn't unusually large, although it was different in at least one other way from most people's; more about that later.)

In any case, it's what's *inside* the brain that counts.

Imagine what it would be like if you could look inside your own brain . . . if you could shut your eyes and peer inward with electron-microscope super-vision . . . closer . . . closer . . . closer at the individual brain cells . . . .Here's some of what you'd see.

Neurons, Axons, and Dendrites

You were born with somewhere between 100 and 200 billion brain cells.

People used to think that the more brain cells you had, the smarter you were, but we now know that this isn't true.

About 10-50 billion of these are nerve cells called *neurons*. A neuron is a basic unit of the brain. Each one is as complex as a small computer. Like a mini-information processing system, it sends and receives thousands of messages in the form of nerve impulses. (A single neuron can handle as many as 50,000 messages per minute!)

Just as no two brains are alike, no two neurons are alike. Each has its own irregular shape, sort of like a tiny octopus with tentacles.

A neuron consists of a cell body (which contains the nucleus), long fibers called *axons*, and short, branching fibers called *dendrites*.

How does it all work?

First, the neuron receives a message. Then it processes the message inside the cell body. Then it sends it out to other neurons by way of the axons.

When a message travels along the length of an axon, it comes close to "touching" the dendrites of the neighboring neurons. But it never *quite* touches. Instead, the message is transmitted chemically across an infinitesimally small gap called a *synapse*.

Is a synapse just a hole in your brain? Hardly. It makes it possible for neurons to communicate with one another. (Think of a synapse as a bridge.) Scientists believe that synapses somehow "decide" whether or not a message gets transmitted. (Now think of it as an "smart" bridge.) They also believe that synapses are where learning and memory occur. So they're *very* important.

A lot of action takes place whenever a message is transmitted. Each message starts off as an electrical impulse. Then it changes into a chemical signal. Then it changes back into an electrical impulse. All within a split second!

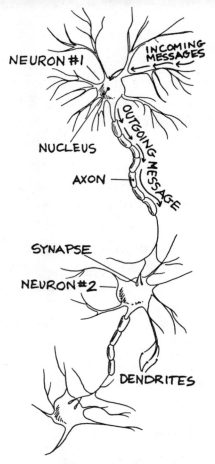

Right now, while you're reading this book, up to *one million* impulses could be flashing through your brain — at speeds of up to 250 miles per hour!

If you want to know more about how your brain sends and receives messages, read:
* *The Brain and Nervous System* by Brian R. Ward (New York: Franklin Watts, 1981).
*** *Brain, Mind, and Behavior* by Floyd E. Bloom, Arlyne Lazerson, and Laura Hofstadter (New York: W.H. Freeman and Company, 1985), chapter 2.

The Cosmic Dance

Remember that you only use a portion of your brain's total capacity. What if you could activate the whole thing at once?

27

Dr. Pyotr Anokhin has tried to calculate the number of synaptic connections possible within a normal human brain. He estimates a total of 1 followed by 6,213,710 miles of typewritten zeros — and he thinks this figure might be too low!

PLUS: Whenever you learn something new, this creates even *more* links between your neurons. The number of neurons stay the same, but they have more ways to share messages.

According to Dr. Barbara Clark, author of *Growing Up Gifted*, a stimulating environment can cause changes in the chemical makeup of the neurons. The strength and speed of the activity at the synapses actually increases. It may be that "smart" people are smart simply because they have better synaptic connections between their brain cells than other people.

An environment full of learning opportunities also affects other brain cells called *glial cells*. These cells "glue" your brain together. Unlike neurons, glial cells can split in two and duplicate themselves. When this happens, axons can push through and make connections to other neurons. The richer your environment, the faster your glial cells split.

(Remember we promised you more on Einstein's brain? Here it is: He had more *glial cells* than most people, so he had more synaptic connections.)

Electrical impulses! Messages coming and going! Multiplying synapses! Splitting cells! And you thought things were pretty quiet up there!

Now imagine that these messages are tiny lights, and that you can see them zipping through your brain. What does it all look like?

A million, billion stars doing a brilliant cosmic dance!

DEFINING INTELLIGENCE

You may think you're smart . . . but you're smarter than you think.

You have the potential for understanding the nature of your own intelligence — and changing it.

There's no limit to how much your brain can learn.

In fact, the more you know, the more you can know!

For decades, the brain has been called "the organ of intelligence." When you hear someone say, "What a brain!" or "She's brainy!", what they usually mean is that the person is smart.

But is "smartness" the same as "intelligence"? Can we define one by the other?

If you're not sure, you're not alone. Scientists are stumped when it comes to deciding on a definition of intelligence — especially *human* intelligence. (Intelligence is usually much easier to recognize than to define.)

Some say it's "the ability to learn and apply what has been learned." But almost every creature on earth — not just humans — can learn and act on the basis of what it learns.

Some say it's "using what has been learned to solve problems." But monkeys can do this, too.

Still others say it's "the ability to judge well, comprehend well, and reason well." Now we're getting somewhere! Most experts agree that our ability to think and reason is what sets us apart from the other animals and makes us special.

One of the most recent definitions states that "intelligence is the result of all the functions of the human brain ... a combination of physical, emotional, mental and spiritual energies." That about covers it.

Robert Sternberg, a leading authority on intelligence, interviewed hundreds of people and asked them what they considered to be the "characteristics of intelligence." He came up with three very general ones:

1 practical problem-solving ability,

2 verbal activity (being able to recognize, understand, and reason with words), and

3 social competence (or "human relations skills" — the ability to communicate with other people).

He also developed his own definition of intelligence: "goal-directed, adapted behavior."

With all these big words bouncing around, it's interesting to find out what kids have to say about intelligence. Over 400 eight-to-sixteen-year-olds gave us their definitions. Here are a few:

To me, intelligence means
being able to stretch
your mind further.
— Don, 11

I'm not sure, but I think it
means being able to learn
things on your own.
Karl, 13

Does it mean being more
logical and highly advanced
— Brenda, 11

Being able to learn, understand
and apply a theory or idea.
Steve, 14

Intelligence is someone like me.
Socky?
age 12

Intelligence is not just
knowledge, but being
able to draw new
conclusions and theories/
ideas from your knowledge.
Andrea, 13

Intelligence is when you're aggressive at everything you do.

Jill, 11

Being able to learn, understand and apply a theory or idea.

Steve, 14

Using your intelligence means you try to be creative and inventive.

Nancy, 16

I think intelligence is the ability to understand and be imaginative.

Julie, 12

Intelligence is the ability to use what you have upstairs.

Justin J. 13

How would *you* define intelligence?

MEASURING INTELLIGENCE

Years ago, someone squeaked out of having to provide a *useful* definition of intelligence by saying, "Intelligence is what intelligence tests measure."

But what do intelligence tests test *for*? And how can we be certain that the tests work if we're not even sure what intelligence *is*?

For many years our society has been more concerned with measuring intelligence than defining it. Let's look at how the whole thing got started . . . and some of the arguments that have come about as a result.

Sir Frances Galton

About 100 years ago, Sir Frances Galton (he was one of Charles Darwin's cousins) began to study human intelligence. He thought that intelligence was something you inherited, like blue eyes or Type O blood, and that the amount of intelligence you were born with stayed the same until you died.

Today we know that this is all baloney.

Alfred Binet

Alfred Binet, a French psychologist, is considered "the father of intelligence testing." In 1905 he and a colleague, Theodore Simon, made up a test that was supposed to show which students would succeed in school and which wouldn't. It was called the "Binet-Simon Scale."

The two men wanted to know things like, "Is a smart 8-year-old as smart as a 9- or 10-year old?" So they designed activities and questions for specific age groups. Their goal was to find out what the "average" child of each age group could do. They determined a child's "mental age" (or MA) by the type of tests the child was able to pass. If a 6-year-old was able to pass the tests meant for 8-year-olds, then they assigned the 6-year-old an MA of 8.

But other psychologists discovered problems with the Binet-Simon scale. Some 16-year-olds scored the same as 10-year-olds — and so did some 5-year-olds. A better, more accurate kind of test was needed.

Wilhelm Stern

In 1912, building on what Binet and Simon and other researchers had done, Wilhelm Stern developed a mathematical equation that could be used to measure a person's "mental quotient." Later on this became known as "intelligence quotient" — **I.Q.**

Here's how it works: Let's say an 8-year-old child passes all the tests meant for 10-year-olds. The child is assigned an MA of 10. Next, the MA is divided by the child's chronological age — 8. Finally, the quotient is then multiplied by 100 to get the child's I.Q. score — in this case, 125.

$$10/8 \times 100 = 125$$

Because most people tested in this way were found to have mental ages very close to their chronological ages, they ended up with I.Q. scores of around 100. So 100 was considered to be the "average" I.Q. for any age.

The I.Q. test proved to be very popular. Millions of people were tested. When the dust settled, about half of them were found to be of "average" intelligence, with I.Q.s between 90 and 110. One-fourth were found to be of "below average" intelligence, with I.Q.s between 60 and 90. And the remaining one-fourth were found to be of "above average" intelligence, with I.Q.s between 110 and 150.

These findings fit neatly onto a bell-shaped curve, like this:

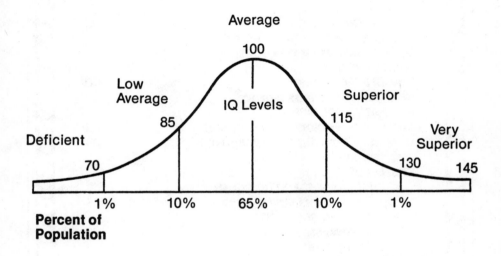

A lot of experts disagreed with what this graph seemed to say (and a lot still do). They argued that you can't measure a person's intelligence this easily, and that the whole concept of mental age is misleading because it implies that two people with the same mental age have the same type of mind.

ESTIMATED I.Q.s OF CELEBRATED PEOPLE

I.Q. tests were all the rage in the early 1900s. In fact, it got so bad that people who had been dead for years (even centuries) were assigned I.Q. scores.

In 1926, for example, a group of psychologists published a study of the most eminent men who had lived between 1450 and 1850. Here are some of them and their *estimated* I.Q.s:

	I.Q.
John Stuart Mill *(English writer and economist)*	190
Johann Wolfgang von Goethe *(German poet)*	185
Voltaire *(French writer)*	170
Wolfgang Amadeus Mozart *(Austrian composer)*	150
Thomas Jefferson *(U.S. President)*	145
Benjamin Franklin *(U.S. diplomat, statesman, and scientist)*	145
Charles Dickens *(English novelist and humorist)*	145
Leonardo da Vinci *(Italian painter, scientist, and engineer)*	135
Sir Isaac Newton *(English mathematician)*	130
George Washington *(first U.S. President)*	125
Johann Sebastian Bach *(German composer)*	125
Rembrandt van Rijn *(Dutch painter)*	110

Excerpt from "The Early Mental Traits of Three Hundred Geniuses" by Catherine Morris Cox, in *Genetic Studies of Genius*, volume II, edited by Lewis M. Terman (Stanford, California: Stanford University Press, 1926). Reprinted by permission of the publisher.

Lewis Terman

In 1916 Lewis Terman, a psychologist at Stanford University in California, took the ideas of Binet and Simon further and developed something called the *Stanford-Binet* test. Today this is the most widely used of all the intelligence tests.

The Stanford-Binet has been revised several times. It includes over 100 subtests and tasks. This may seem like a lot, but each one is quite short: it only takes 60-90 minutes to complete the entire test. How many subtests and tasks a person is asked to do depends on how old he or she is.

The Stanford-Binet has been widely used for nearly 70 years. Many people like it — and many people don't. Some think it puts too much emphasis on verbal and rote memory. Others think that a single score (which is all you get) can't possibly represent all of the complex thinking functions. Still others point out that it doesn't measure creativity and isn't suitable for adults.

In spite of such criticism, the Stanford-Binet is believed to be a good way of measuring "general intelligence."

David Wechsler

Some of the newest intelligence tests were designed by psychologist David Wechsler in the 1930s, 40s, and 50s. Today they are in use all over the country.

Wechsler felt that finding out a person's MA wasn't enough to determine his or her I.Q. So he used mental age "equivalents" as guides, not as the last word.

The first Wechsler Intelligence Scale for Children (WISC) was published in 1949. The revised version (WISC-R) came out in 1974 and has proved very popular.

If you've been wearing your thinking cap while you've been reading this, you may have been wondering, "What's the difference between an *intelligence* test and an *achievement* test?"

Well, both kinds measure aptitude, learning, and achievement to some degree. But an intelligence test does more. It taps into a wider range of life experiences and looks for whether you apply what you know in new and different ways.

An achievement test, on the other hand, tries to discover the facts you've learned at home and at school. A reading test and a math test are both examples of achievement tests.

Which would *you* rather take?

THE TROUBLE WITH INTELLIGENCE TESTS

There *does* seem to be some connection between a person's I.Q. and how "smart" he or she is. For example, psychologists have found that people with higher I.Q.s can process information and come up with responses more quickly than people with lower I.Q.s.

Scientists have based countless conclusions on the results of intelligence tests. And educators have used these results in making decisions about students.

But the tests aren't perfect. In fact, there's a lot wrong with them.

Maybe you've taken a group intelligence test in school. Instead of an I.Q. score, you received a percentile score. Maybe you and your parents and your teachers believed that this score told all about you and your brain.

Unfortunately, your score may have been influenced by things *outside* your head — things you had no control over. For example: Did someone read the test directions aloud? The *way* that person read the directions (emphasizing some words over others, maybe even getting some wrong) may have affected your score and the scores of everyone around you.

Was the test multiple choice? Did you guess at some of the answers? Guessing isn't a very good indicator of what you really know.

What if you're a super-creative person who finds more than one answer for a question? You could be penalized for this.

How well a person does on an intelligence test often depends on how well he or she speaks English. But what about people for whom English is a second language . . . or those who are just learning English? In these cases, is the test fair?

You probably took a *standardized* test. Standardized means that the test must first be tried out on groups of subjects from different age, income, and intelligence levels. But this trying-out process takes time . . . sometimes years. So your test may have been outdated.

Can a paper-and-pencil test measure *all* of your brain-related abilities? What if you're good at baseball? What if you're a terrific singer? What if you stole the show in the last class play? What if you're the best babysitter in your neighborhood? These kinds of things never show up on intelligence tests.

The controversy goes on and on. Do the tests contain too much cultural bias? How do they account for genetic and environmental differences? Are they socially and racially fair, or do they favor a particular group? Which of the 200 tests available is the *best* one?

If these tests have so many problems, why do people keep taking (and giving) them?

For one reason, old habits die hard. Our schools are used to testing. They think that test scores can predict a student's future success — even though no one has ever proved this! Still, colleges base admissions decisions at least partly on student test scores. And some employers refer to them when making hiring decisions.

There *is* one thing these tests are good for: predicting how well a person will do on later tests! That's because taking an intelligence test is like a game. The more times you "play" it, the better you get and the more little "tricks" you learn.

Okay, maybe there's one more thing: Many educators use tests for *diagnostic purposes*. The tests point out students' strengths and weaknesses, and the teachers can then teach to those strengths and weaknesses.

But what do intelligence tests do for *you*? Not much, as it turns out.

An I.Q. score (or a percentile score) doesn't even scratch the surface of your capabilities. You have too many talents that don't relate to it. (Like baseball, singing, acting, babysitting.)

No intelligence test can begin to show how sensitive, creative, likeable or happy you are. It won't measure how eager you are to learn.

In other words, if you *do* take an I.Q. test, *don't take the results that seriously*! And don't bother to cram ahead of time with any of the hundreds of books on the market which promise to "raise" your I.Q. There's no secret formula that can do that.

What if you do practice and end up with a higher score? Big deal. That won't make you any smarter.

Besides, *it's not important*. What *is* important is that you can always keep on learning, every day for the rest of your life.

"The best way to find out if you can achieve something is to try to achieve it."

—**Arthur Jensen** (*it's strange that he said this, because this famous scholar of heredity believed that intelligence depends on genes*)

If you want to know more about intelligence testing, read:
* *You're Smarter Than You Think* by Linda Perigo Moore (New York: Holt, Rinehart and Winston, 1985).
*** *The Mismeasure of Man* by Stephen Jay Gould (New York: W.W. Norton & Co., 1981).

NATURE VS. NURTURE

Have you ever wondered where your intelligence came from? Was it passed down to you in the genes you inherited from your parents? Or is it a result of your environment — the things and people and influences and stimuli around you?

Although scientists and scholars have been asking these questions for years, nobody has yet come up with THE answer. That's why this whole issue is called the "nature vs. nurture controversy."

Here's what we do know (or think we know!) so far:

- Your physical, mental, and emotional characteristics are a result of *both* your heredity and your environment.

- No two people have exactly the same genes (not even identical twins).

- No two people have exactly the same environment. (Remember that environment involves all sorts of things, including the way people interact with you. Even siblings raised in the same family will be treated somewhat differently by their parents, have different experiences at home and at school, and so on.)

■ No two people perceive and respond to their environment in exactly the same way.

■ What a person becomes, and the abilities he or she develops, often depends on how strongly genes and environment *complement* each other.

We might put this last idea in terms of two very general equations:

great genes + great environment = the best chance of success

awful genes + awful environment = uh-oh!

BUT: these equations sometimes add up to the *opposite* answers. Some people who have the best of everything all their lives turn out to be real duds. Other people who start out with nothing can overcome their heredity and their environment to accomplish almost anything they set out to do.

■ Research has shown that heredity can determine how your brain will react to your environment. Similarly, the quality of your environment can affect your mental abilities.

Can we draw any conclusions from what we've learned about the nature vs. nurture controversy? The most obvious is: we still have a *lot* to learn about where intelligence comes from. The most encouraging is: what you do with what you have is up to you.

MULTIPLE INTELLIGENCES

The nature vs. nurture controversy has been raging for quite a while, and there's no sign that it will let up anytime soon. But that's not the only thing brain experts are arguing about.

Thanks to the brain, people are coming up with new ideas about intelligence all the time. One of the most fascinating is the notion of *multiple intelligences*.

Two of the best-known names associated with this most recent debate are Yale psychologist Robert Sternberg (we've mentioned him earlier, in the "Defining Intelligence" section) and Harvard psychologist Howard Gardner. Let's find out what each has to say.

Robert Sternberg

Sternberg believes that "real life" is where intelligence is at. He sees intelligence as a mental activity, or process, that people can be taught. In other words, he doesn't view intelligence as a "built-in" thing that you either have or don't have.

In his book, *Beyond I.Q.: A Triarchic Theory of Human Intelligence*, Sternberg defines three types of intelligence.

1 **Contextual intelligence** is the intelligence you use when you adapt to your environment, change your environment, or select a different environment to suit your needs.

2 **Experiential intelligence** is the intelligence you use whenever you build on your experience to solve problems in new situations.

3 **Internal intelligence** is the intelligence you use to approach a problem and evaluate the feedback to determine whether you should change your approach.

Sternberg has coined another term — "tacit knowledge" — to refer to "the things you need to know to succeed, but which are not necessarily taught or verbalized." For example, you call on your tacit knowledge when you're planning how to best use your time or resources. This kind of knowledge you have to pick up on your own.

According to Sternberg, intelligence can be enhanced. Like many of his colleagues, he's convinced that we don't even come close to our true potential. But as more and more people start believing that they *can* succeed, it's very likely that they *will* succeed.

Howard Gardner

Gardner approaches the issue of multiple intelligences from another perspective. He thinks that it's too limiting to focus on the mind alone. In his book, *Frames of Mind: The Theory of Multiple Intelligences*, he lists *six* different kinds of human intelligence.

1 **Linguistic intelligence** enables you to write, listen, and speak. It means choosing the right words and being sensitive to the many ways in which language is used. Poets, novelists, and public speakers have lots of linguistic intelligence.

2 **Musical intelligence** is the earliest to emerge. (Think of musical prodigies like Mozart, who began his career as a performer and a composer at age 3!) It means being able to "hear" music and make sense out of pitch, rhythm, and musical sequences. Composers, musicians, singers, and dancers rely on their musical intelligence — and they may all use it in different ways.

3 **Logical-mathematical intelligence** makes it possible for you to put objects in some kind of order and to comprehend quantities. When you were younger, you used to do this mainly with physical objects (like blocks), but now you can probably do it in your head, too. Mathematicians and scientists display this kind of intelligence when they go through long "chains" of reasoning.

4 **Spatial intelligence** enables you to perceive a form or an object, see the world accurately, and mentally "rotate" complex forms and imagine how they'll look when you turn them around. Visual perception and the ability to draw are part of it. Sculptors, inventors, engineers, painters, and chess players have high spatial intelligence.

5 **Bodily-kinesthetic intelligence** is what makes you good at handling objects or controlling your physical movements. Dancers, mime artists, swimmers, actors, ball players, and inventors have plenty of it.

6 **Personal intelligence** helps you to understand yourself and others. It enables you to examine your own feelings and distinguish them from other people's. You use this intelligence to "key in" on other people's moods, temperaments, and intentions. Psychologists, counselors, teachers, and salespeople need this kind of intelligence.

Gardner believes that all six intelligences function independently but can be closely related. He also believes that when one or two are especially strong they can "lead" a person in a certain direction.

What are your talents? Which of the six intelligences can you attribute them to?

Plus Gardner believes that each intelligence has its own "life history." An intelligence may "bloom" briefly and then fade away.

What if we could learn to hold onto them all? What if we could learn to improve on those we're weak at? What if we could find a way to "tap into" different ones at different times?

TWO BRAINS ARE BETTER THAN ONE

W.J., a World War II soldier, was hit in the head with a rifle. The blow damaged W.J.'s brain and caused him to have seizures.

Meanwhile, back in California, a team of surgeons led by Dr. Roger Sperry was trying to figure out a way to control seizures in brain-damaged people and epileptics. They devised the concept of "split-brain" surgery. W.J. became their first patient.

Early in the 1960s, Dr. Joseph Bogen, a neurosurgeon, took a piece of piano wire and sliced through W.J.'s corpus callosum — the thick bundle of nerves connecting the right and left hemispheres of the brain. The surgery successfully isolated the hemispheres, and from then on W.J.'s seizures occurred in only one hemisphere rather than both.

From tests they performed on W.J. and other patients, Sperry and his team learned that the corpus callosum is a communications network which relays information back and forth between the brain's two hemispheres. (Today we know that the corpus callosum carries about four *billion* messages per second.) Severing it enabled them to study the separate functions of each side of the brain and draw conclusions about which functions were housed where.

You know by now that brain research is almost always controversial. The work of Sperry and his team was no exception. A lot of people disagreed with their findings.

Some argued that they were invalid because the experiments were done on patients whose brains were injured or damaged. Others pointed out that different patients performed differently after surgery. Still others noted that the research of Sperry and his associates focused only on the cerebral hemispheres while ignoring the other regions of the brain, including the lobes and the cortices.

But many people have jumped on the bandwagon and wholeheartedly support the theory of left- and right-brain specialization. And it does appear that each hemisphere is in charge of certain things.

This doesn't mean what some people think it does, however. For example, you may have heard that "analytical thinking is in the left hemisphere." Wrong! It isn't *in* it at all. Rather, the left hemisphere seems to *process* analytical thinking more efficiently than the right hemisphere.

Or you may have heard that "imagination is in the right hemisphere." Wrong again! Instead, the right hemisphere seems to specialize in a form of *processing* that is capable of fantasy and dreams.

These distinctions are important. So, too, is the fact that they may not apply to everybody. Remember that no two brains are alike, and that no two function in exactly the same ways. Our brains are as individual as our thumbprints.

Still, there *are* some aspects of the left-brain/right-brain theory that most scientists seem to agree on. One is that the left hemisphere controls the right side of the body while the right hemisphere controls the left.

Professor Robert Ornstein has found that in most (not all) cases the left hemisphere controls these functions: *language* (speech, facts, names and dates, spelling); *linear, sequential thinking* (processing information one step at a time); *literal thinking* (understanding the literal meanings of words); *logical thinking*; *mathematical thinking* (numbers and their relationships); *reasoning*; and *analysis*.

The right brain controls these functions: *simultaneous processing* (processing different kinds of information at the same time and seeing the "big picture"); *imagination* (fantasies, dreams, daydreams); the sense of *color* (distinguishing colors, artistic abilities); *musical abilities* and the awareness of *rhythm*; *emotions*; the ability to see *patterns* and *relationships*; *spatial tasks*; *intuition*; and the understanding of *metaphor* (the difference between what's said and what's meant).

Adding up a list of numbers is a left-brain activity. In other words, while you're doing this your left brain shows more awareness and your right brain "rests."

Putting together a jigsaw puzzle and arranging colored blocks are right-brain activities. During these, your left brain "rests."

Most of the time, though, our left and right brains work together, sharing responsibilities and integrating streams of thought.

Here are some examples of how they cooperate:

■ When you sing a song, the right hemisphere maintains a sense of melody and rhythm while the left supplies the words and operates your vocal apparatus.

■ When you write a description of a work of art, you begin by looking at it (right brain). But as soon as you start to write the left brain takes over.

■ When you solve a problem, the left brain does the deductive reasoning while the right brain contributes intuition and insight.

51

Throughout history, many significant creative discoveries have been made by people who used *both* sides of their brains.

☐ Leonardo da Vinci not only excelled in math, language, logical thinking and analytical thinking; he was also great at using imagination, color, rhythm, and form.

☐ Albert Einstein discovered the Theory of Relativity by fantasizing what it would be like to ride a beam of light into space. Ideas came to him as pictures and images, and he then put them into words. (He once said, "My gift of fantasy has meant more to me than my talent for absorbing positive knowledge.")

☐ Charles Schulz of *Peanuts* fame used drawing to express almost any thought on any subject. A keen observer, he continually "drew" with his eyes.

☐ Steve Allen uses free association and dreams to create his books, songs, and albums. According to him, "a dream is like 827 moments of creativity all scotch-taped together."

Two brains *are* better than one!

If you want to know more about left-brain/right-brain theories and findings, read:
** *Drawing on the Right Side of the Brain* by Better Edwards (Los Angeles: J.P. Tarcher, Inc., 1979).
*** *Left Brain, Right Brain* by Sally P. Springer and Georg Deutsch (San Francisco: W.H. Freeman and Co., 1981).

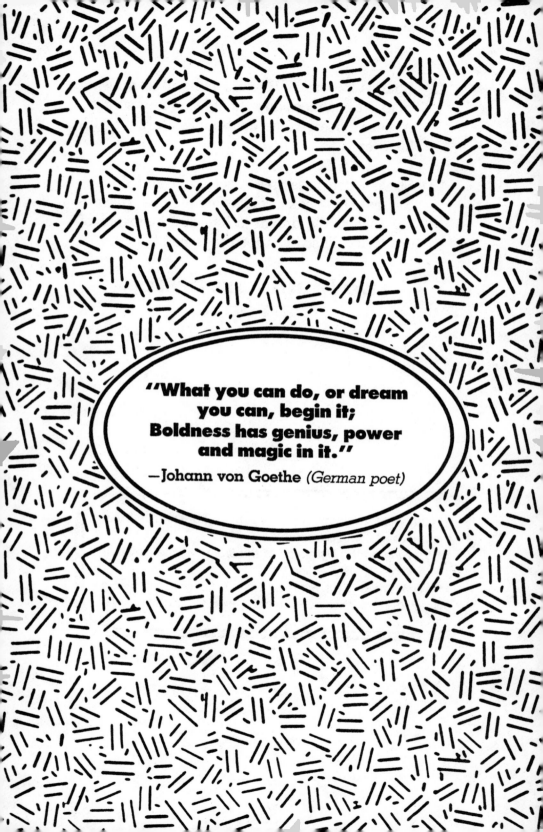

"What you can do, or dream you can, begin it; Boldness has genius, power and magic in it."

—Johann von Goethe (German poet)

SEX AND THE BRAIN

It's time to ask the question everyone has been waiting for: Who's smarter, boys or girls?

In other words, are there any differences between the female brain and the male brain? If so, what are they?

It used to be that psychologists hesitated to investigate these issues because they didn't want to upset anyone. The mere thought that one sex might be "superior" to the other made people mad.

But we can't escape the fact that there *are* differences between the sexes. Once we accept that, we can go on to explore them and add to our knowledge.

For example: We know that, on average, male brains weigh slightly more than female brains. The brain's weight as a percentage of total body weight is about the same for both sexes, however.

We also know that males show more variability in intelligence than females. This means that there are more males than females with very high I.Q.s — and more males than females with very *low* I.Q.s. Thus, while there are more male than female geniuses in the arts and sciences, there are also more males with mental disorders.

Why? No one knows for sure, but it could have something to do with the fact that in males the two hemispheres of the brain seem more specialized. In contrast, infant girls are born with a more highly developed cortex and a larger corpus callosum. They're able to integrate both sides of the brain to perform a task. Later in life, females tend to solve problems using several different approaches, while males seem more single-minded.

Researchers have concluded that the structure of male brains makes them better at spatial tasks, like stacking colored blocks or putting things together. Dr. Julian Stanley of Johns Hopkins University thinks that this may be why males show stronger mathematical ability than females.

But there are females who have *excellent* spatial ability and males who have *poor* spatial ability. And there are female math whizzes.

Some researchers suggest that males have more highly developed motor skills and are better than females at solving problems involving the manipulation of objects (like jigsaw puzzles). Boys seem to be more interested than girls in how things work, and they generally display more curiosity. They're also more impulsive and more easily distracted. They take more risks, and they're more aggressive.

Females appear to have more highly developed language skills and are better than males at controlling the fine hand movements needed for tasks like penmanship. They're less easily distracted, and they generally process information faster than males. Girls tend to be more interested than boys in people and social relationships, and they have an easier time remembering names and faces. Many girls have a stronger sense of odor, taste, and touch.

Now for the $100,000 question: Which of these differences are physiological, and which are due to environmental influences? If this sounds familiar, it should; we're right back with our old friend, the nature vs. nurture controversy.

Many people today believe that a lot of these differences would disappear if boys and girls were treated the same by their parents from the beginning. Society's expectations and cultural values can affect how we learn and what we learn from the people around us.

Studies have shown that many girls are taught to be passive and nurturing, while many boys are taught to be risk-takers and independent. Often without realizing it, parents encourage these tendencies by the types of clothing and toys they provide and the activities they allow their children to participate in. Later in life, boys are encouraged to do well in school while girls learn that it isn't "ladylike" to be smart.

Often females end up in a double bind, afraid to fail *and* afraid to succeed. One interesting study found that when girls do fail they tend to blame it on themselves or their intellectual inadequacies. But when boys fail they say it's because they weren't motivated or didn't put forth the effort.

Why is it that girls are usually ahead of boys in grade school and start falling behind in high school? Why do females lack confidence and underestimate their abilities, while boys keep raising their expectations of themselves?

Think about these questions. Then remind yourself that you deserve *every* possible chance to develop your abilities and be what *you* want to be!

If you want to know more about sex and the brain, read:
** *Sex and the Brain* by Jo Durden-Smith and Diane de Simone (New York: Warner Books, 1983).

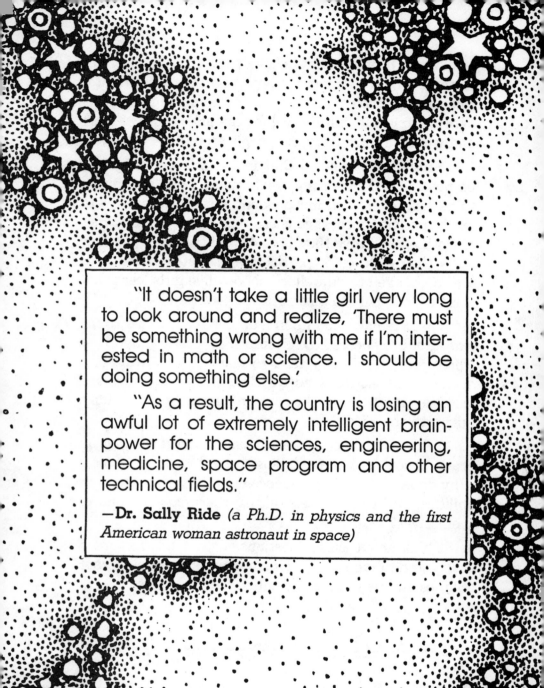

"It doesn't take a little girl very long to look around and realize, 'There must be something wrong with me if I'm interested in math or science. I should be doing something else.'

"As a result, the country is losing an awful lot of extremely intelligent brainpower for the sciences, engineering, medicine, space program and other technical fields."

—**Dr. Sally Ride** *(a Ph.D. in physics and the first American woman astronaut in space)*

WHAT MAKES A PERSON A GENIUS?

In order to be called a genius, a person usually has to accomplish something terrific. In other words, genius should not be equated with I.Q., although most geniuses do come from the high end of the I.Q. distribution.

If the two were the same, however, then everyone with an I.Q. over 150 would be a genius. But there are plenty of high-I.Q. people sitting around doing nothing. (Even the bell curve you saw on page 35 defines this category as "possible" — not "guaranteed" — genius.)

Nobody knows how and why some people become geniuses. But almost all geniuses have at least two things in common: They're *very* strongly motivated to achieve a goal or goals, and they feel secure and confident from childhood through adulthood.

Geniuses can be defined as people who have a knack for getting the most mileage out of their brains — people like Leonardo da Vinci, Mozart, Marie Curie, Thomas Edison, Margaret Mead, Steve Jobs, Walt Disney, Steve Allen, and Pablo Picasso. Most of the time, they're not even sure how they do it.

"I believe that instinct is what makes a genius a genius."

—**Bob Dylan** (*American singer and songwriter*)

You've probably read stories about "child geniuses" or "prodigies." These are the kids who can type and compose poetry at age 3, read the encyclopedia at age 4, speak eight different languages by age 5, and/or start teaching math at a university at age 15. Phew!

What's the cause of their remarkable development? Scientists believe it has something to do with being stimulated and encouraged at an early age. Apparently it's also related to the genes they inherit.

But again, not *everybody* who grows up in an "enhanced" environment turns out to be a genius. Neither does *everybody* with great genes. Neither does *everybody* who has both.

Benjamin Bloom recently conducted a study to find out how 120 of the nation's top artists, athletes, and scholars had become so successful. He and his team of researchers learned that not all of their subjects had what could be called "natural talent." But they *did* all have drive and determination.

For example, a famous concert pianist practiced several hours a day for 17 years to accomplish his goal, and an Olympic swimmer got up at 5:30 every morning to swim two hours before school started. Then she swam another two hours after school was over.

Plus they all had *potential.* And this is something none of us lacks. No matter where we're born, where we live, or whose genes we inherit.

"We must believe that we are gifted for something, and that this thing, at whatever cost, must be obtained."

—**Marie Curie** (*Polish scientist and the first person to win two Nobel prizes; along with her husband, she discovered radioactivity, which led to radiation treatment for cancer*)

PROBLEM SOLVING

Everyone has problems. And most kids have problems like these: "What should I wear today?" "How can I bring up my grade in this class?" "How can I earn more money?" "What can I write about for my term paper?" "What should I do on Saturday night?" "How can I get my little brother to stop bugging me?"

Luckily, you have what you need to solve almost every problem you'll encounter during your lifetime: your brain!

As you probably already know, successful problem solving takes more than just gathering information. Sometimes you have to take a whole new approach — one you haven't tried before. Sometimes you have to stand back and try looking at the problem from different angles.

Think about how you would go about solving this problem:

The day before an important math test, your best friend tells you that her big brother has given her a copy of the one the teacher gave last year. She has already studied it and is willing to share it with you. You know that the test doesn't change much from one year to the next. And you're worried about passing, since math is your worst subject.

What will you tell your friend?

What will you do with the knowledge that your friend is cheating?

Of course, it's easier to solve a hypothetical problem like this one than to deal with the real thing. What was the last genuine problem *you* solved? How did you do it? What thinking process did you use to arrive at a solution? Were you satisfied with the way you handled it? How would you do it if you could do it over?

TEN TERRIFIC TIPS FOR MAKING LIFE EASIER

- Don't assume that all problems are negative. Try viewing some as opportunities to use your brain and take positive action.

- Separate problems into categories. Which are related to goals in your life? Which are a result of being disorganized, or of not planning ahead?

- Break problems down into as many elements as possible. Then break these elements down into steps. Then take each step one at a time.

- Distinguish *real* problems from *fantasy* problems — ones you've made up in your head. Maybe you're just imagining that a problem exists. Unnecessary worrying is a waste of brain power!

- Work backwards. Don't focus only on the solution — the best one may not be obvious at the beginning. Instead, focus on the problem-solving process.

- When faced with a particularly sticky problem, outline it on paper first. List the things you *want to do* about it. Then list the things you *can do* about it. Do the two lists match up?

- Gather information. If any of your friends have dealt with similar problems, find out what they did. And don't hesitate to ask your parents for advice. It's hard to believe, but they used to be your age, and they may have lots of helpful suggestions.

- Develop backup plans. If things don't turn out the way you want them to, what will you do then?

- Be flexible in the way you approach problem solving. Most of us develop problem-solving styles that turn into habits: we approach problems in the same old way, time after time. Maybe you need a change.

- Don't be afraid to "talk to yourself." Some of the most successful problems-solvers think aloud.

If you want to know more about problem-solving techniques, read:
* *The All New Universal Traveler* by Don Koberg and Jim Bagnall (Los Altos, California: William Kaufman, Inc., 1981).
* *A Whack on the Side of the Head* by Roger von Oech, Ph.D. (New York: Warner Books, 1983.)

convergent

open-ended

pattern

sequential

imaginative

divergent

concrete

evaluative

metaphorical

vertica

THOUGHTS ABOUT THINKING

$$3 + 4 = \boxed{?}$$

$$\square\,\bigcirc\,\triangle\,\square\,\bigcirc\,\triangle\,\square \;\; \underline{?}$$

$$3, \; 6, \; 9, \; 12, \;\; \boxed{?}$$

Before you realized that these three lines were problems-to-be-solved, you were already *thinking* about them.

From birth (and maybe before), we humans are blessed with the fantastic ability to think. We do it constantly. Sometimes we're aware (conscious) of our mental activities, and other times we're unaware (unconscious) of them. Most thinking is automatic and takes place below the conscious level. It's a natural process, like breathing.

Consider some of the different kinds of thinking we do:

logical

intuitive   conscious

subconscious   abstract   logical   abstract

nonlinear   conscious   lateral   divergent   lateral

problem-solving   concrete   linear   linear

A lot of these overlap. Even so, thinking about so many types of thinking can boggle the mind!

Now consider the fact that we can think in several ways and about several things at once. You can talk on the telephone and comb your hair . . . listen to the radio and do your homework . . . watch TV and work on a science project . . . read a book and eat lunch . . . doodle on your folder during a boring history lesson . . . .

Thinking is a personal and private process. Because no two brains are exactly alike, no two people think exactly alike — even when they're in the same place and doing the same things.

Try this the next time you have a friend over: Get pencils and paper for both of you, sit down together at a table, and spend five minutes writing down whatever thoughts run through your heads. Then compare what you've written. You'll be amazed!

Some people are afraid to think. Some people are better thinkers than others. What a lot of people don't realize is that *thinking is a skill*. It can be wasted — or it can be improved.

Let's look closely at some of the different kinds of thinking and how *you* can get better at them.

Imagination and Visualization

Thinking is more than just absorbing information. It involves a variety of mental activities. Most of these fit into the category of *imagination*.

Albert Einstein, one of the all-time champion thinkers, once said that "imagination is more important than knowledge." He valued his ability to visualize and create images. Many of his most important discoveries and equations came from this source.

Imagination has been called "the essential tool of human intelligence." With it, we can invent new realities. We can form mental images of something without sensing it and sometimes without ever having seen it before. We can make up characters and look into the future. We can bring the past back to life. There's no limit to what the imagination can do!

Imagined images aren't tied to any specific reference point. They can come from anywhere and lead anywhere you want them to. Your unconscious mind is a storehouse of thousands of images.

How can you tap into them? Sometimes the best way to do this is *not to try*. Just relax! Many people get their brightest ideas (the "Ahas!") while riding in a car, walking, bathing or showering, reading, listening to music, or dropping off to sleep. When do you get yours?

Imagined images don't always take the form of mental pictures. In fact, only one person out of four is capable of making good mental pictures. This doesn't mean that the other three have poor imaginations. They may be able to imagine touches, sounds, body feelings, or abstract concepts instead.

To find out more about how your imagination works, try putting yourself inside these scenes:

● You're part of a team that's just climbed Mount Everest.

● You've been chosen to lead the next Space Shuttle launch.

● You're a famous rock star about to go on stage at Yankee Stadium.

● You're an Egyptian pharaoh.

Can you "see" yourself in each situation? Describe your surroundings. What can you smell, taste, "feel"? What are you wearing? What's going on around you?

Your imagination may be all in your head, but its effects are often felt throughout your body. To find out how, try these imaging exercises:

 You take a big, juicy lemon out of the refrigerator, cut it into quarters, bring one quarter toward your mouth . .and sink your teeth into it.

 You sense the presence of something on your arm. You look down and see a big, creepy spider slowly making its way toward your shoulder.

 You're crouched in the open door of a plane, wearing a parachute. You're thousands of feet above the ground and the wind is howling around you. Someone gives you a shove — and out you go!

Did thinking about the lemon get your salivary glands going? Did thinking about the spider send shivers down your spine? Did thinking about jumping out of a plane cause your heart to beat faster or your breathing to accelerate?

Some people's imaginations roam most freely when they're most relaxed — flat on their backs and sound asleep. When we dream, our imagination takes center stage. We'll talk more about dreaming later. (If you can't wait, turn to page 119.)

Logical Thinking

"I have track practice after school today. Guess I'll take my track shoes with me."

Makes sense, right? So does most of the logical thinking we do. And we do so much of it during a normal day that we're hardly even aware of it.

Nobody knows exactly how logical thinking works, but it seems to be related to the ways in which we organize and associate ideas. It's believed to be a function of the left brain.

When we think logically, we begin with certain assumptions and concepts. Then we generate ideas, step by step, until we arrive at an "end point" or, if we're thinking about a problem, a solution. Much of this step-by-step thinking goes on below the conscious level.

For example, several distinct thoughts may take place in between "I have track practice after school today" and "Guess I'll take my track shoes with me." Some of these may include, "Track practice . . . that means running . . . that means feet on cinders . . . need to protect feet . . . need special shoes . . . track shoes . . . know where they are . . . get them out of closet and put them by door so I won't forget them."

The conscious part of your brain "leaps" over these intermediate steps to reach a conclusion. And it happens very quickly — almost instantaneously.

Even though logical thinking often occurs naturally, without our knowing it, it's something we can get better at — and *should* get better at. Why? Because each day we're bombarded with tons of information coming at us from all directions: TV, radio, magazines, newspapers, school, conversations with parents and friends, and on and on. We need to know what's important, what's not, what we need, what we can do without, what to store and what to ignore. If we didn't make these distinctions, our thinking would degenerate into nonsense. "I have track practice after school today. Guess I'll take my pet alligator with me" wouldn't get you very far!

Actually, logical thinking is a pretty straightforward process. Most of the time it involves making conclusions based on certain known facts. Here's a simple logical argument you're probably familiar with:

All A's are B's
All B's are C's
Therefore, all A's are C's.

But even with this simple three-step process, you have to be careful. If your facts aren't correct, it won't work! **For example:**

All basketball players are tall.
All tall people are funny.
Therefore, all basketball players are funny.

The trouble with this line of reasoning is that it isn't based on truths. All basketball players *aren't* tall (even though most of them are). And all tall people *aren't* funny (even though some of them are). So unless you're talking about the Harlem Globetrotters, this argument is a wash!

Use this pattern to make up your own logical argument. But be careful with your facts!

All _____ are _____ .
All _____ are _____ .
Therefore, all _____ are _____ .

Another example of a logical argument goes like this:

All B's are C.
A is a C.
Therefore, A is a B.

Or, in other words:

All cars have four wheels.
A Ford Fiesta has four wheels.
Therefore, a Ford Fiesta is a car.

So far, so good. But what about this?

All cars have four wheels.
A skateboard has four wheels.
Therefore, a skateboard is a car.

The first argument is correct; the second is false. Can you see why?

Logical thinking involves making assumptions — but sometimes we can't assume too much!

One way of understanding logical thinking is by looking at how *illogical* it can be. Here's another silly example:

I like caramel corn and green grapes.

I am a good student.

Therefore, anyone who doesn't like caramel corn and green grapes isn't a good student.

Sometimes logical fallacies aren't this easy to spot. It takes a keen observer to analyze a supposedly logical thinking process and discover the flaws.

This, too, is something you can get better at — with practice. The next time you're watching a TV newscast or reading the newspaper, see if you can pick out an example of illogical thinking in the information being presented. You may be very surprised at what you discover!

How can you avoid "crooked" thinking? By checking your facts, avoiding unfounded assumptions, and paying attention to what you see and hear. Try not to get "trapped" by arguments that only *seem* logical.

Intuition

Intuition isn't a mysterious talent reserved for only a few special people. In fact, it's almost impossible *not* to be intuitive. The trick lies in being sensitive to what our intuition tell us — and knowing when it's steering us in the wrong direction.

How many times have you said, "I have a hunch that this is the right answer," or "I have a gut feeling about this"? How often have you sensed someone walking up behind you before you heard footsteps? How often have you known what someone else was thinking or feeling? In each case, your intuition was at work.

Where does intuition come from? Past experience, mostly. The things we've done or observed before collect in our minds until some situations seem "familiar" and we know what to expect from them.

Intuition has been called the "sixth sense." We can hear it and clearly understand it. It often speaks to us on a physical level. If we're about to be sick, our intuition helps us find ways to relieve our discomfort.

Athletes are always using their intuition. They don't have time to think about every move and play, so they rely on their subconscious to tell them what to do.

How much should *you* trust *your* intuition? That's the same as asking how much you should trust your logical thinking. Either one can fool you. Often the two work best when they're used together. Start by carefully studying a situation, and then let your intuition guide you toward your final conclusion or decision.

How can you improve your intuitive powers? No one really knows, since intuition doesn't seem to be something you can practice. But people who are especially intuitive share certain characteristics, like patience, humility, self-control, and the ability to relax.

Incidentally, intuition doesn't seem to be related to a person's sex, no matter how much you may have heard about "women's intuition." Lots of males are intuitive, too.

Daydreaming

We all know what daydreaming is. It's that marvelous ability to take a mind-trip away from where we are to someplace we'd rather be.

In the middle of math class, you daydream about the carnival you went to last weekend . . . while you're washing dishes, you daydream about the new stereo system you're saving up to buy.

Daydreaming is a special kind of thinking. It combines memory, imagination, and intuition. Like the dreams we have while we're asleep, a daydream may involve scenes, objects, and people we know and don't know. The difference between daydreams and night dreams is that we can control the former.

Almost everybody daydreams, but very few people know how to *use* this ability to their advantage. Daydreaming can help us to solve problems and become more creative. Unfortunately, it's usually not welcome in school. Because students usually get scolded for not paying attention, many never discover that they can use their daydreams to generate new ideas.

It would be great if we could somehow convince our teachers and parents that daydreaming can be good for us. Any ideas?

Your daydreams are like movies, and you're the director. Studies have shown that about 96% of all people daydream at some time or another — about success, about failure, about going on adventures, about people they know or would like to know. As kids become more aware of the opposite sex, they tend to spend a lot of time on romantic daydreams. Your daydreams can take you wherever you want to go!

To improve your daydreaming skills, try setting aside a half-hour each day when there's nothing else you have to do. Get comfortable and turn your mind loose. Afterward, think about where your daydreaming led you.

Pattern Thinking

Ever since you were born, sensory stimuli have been tracing "patterns" in your brain tissue — almost like road maps. The messages you've received through your sight, hearing, touch, smelling, and tasting have been organized into patterns and stamped into your brain.

These mental patterns are useful — actually, *essential* — because they help you to recognize familiar objects and circumstances. You know what to do without having to stop and figure it out. We all rely on pattern thinking, even though we're usually unaware of it.

Pattern thinking is what tells you that a cat is a cat, not a camel. It's what helps you to recognize your parents, your friends, your teachers, your neighbors. It lets you know that a fork is for eating with, not scratching with. It teaches you to stop on red and go on green.

Pattern thinking can enhance the efficiency of all our perceptual processes, especially our visualization and organization skills. Unfortunately, it can also get us stuck in a rut. Once you get used to one pattern, it's hard to go beyond it.

Take a look at this picture:

What do you see? A vase or a face? If you've never seen this picture before, you may have noticed *both*, shifting back and forth until you settled on one. But if you *have* seen this picture before, chances are you see the same thing now that you saw back then. It's hard to get beyond a pattern you're used to.

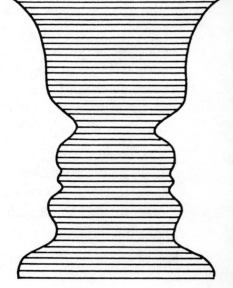

74

You can force yourself to break or change a pattern. Try it right now by looking at the picture again. If you see a face, make yourself see a vase. If you see a vase, make yourself see a face. **Remember: it's all in your head!**

Think Positively!

Unless you've been living in a cave for the past ten years, you've heard about the power of positive thinking. People who have it claim that it works miracles. And they may be right!

Positive thinking means making your brain work *for* you rather than *against* you. It involves seeing things positively and using positive words to express your thoughts and feelings. In a way, it's a form of self-hypnosis. (For more about self-hypnosis, see page 115.)

It's so simple, it's almost scary. Tell yourself that you're terrible at geometry, and you probably will be. But tell yourself that you're getting better at it every day and you will!

Positive thinking focuses on success. Positive thinkers don't program themselves *not to lose*; they program themselves to *win*. They don't program themselves *not to be dull*; they program themselves to *be alert*. There's a big difference.

Think of a class you wish you could do better in. Start telling yourself, every day, "This is an interesting class. I'm starting to like it more. I can do well here." Just saying these words will make you feel more optimistic. Thinking positively can go a long way toward helping you achieve your goals.

If negative thoughts do start creeping into your mind, try getting rid of them like this: Imagine yourself kicking them out! Put them into a mental picture of a creature you despise (like a monster — or a cockroach).

75

This will arouse your feelings of aggression, and you'll be able to envision yourself giving the creature the boot.

Another way to increase your power of positive thinking is by cutting negative phrases out of your vocabulary. Like these:

"I hate ... "   *"I can't ... "*

"I'm sick of ... "   *"I'm afraid of ... "*

"That's impossible ... "   *"I'll probably blow it ... "*

"That'll never work ... " *"Everything I do turns out wrong ... "*

What others do *you* use that belong on this list? Write them down on a piece of paper. Then tear it up and throw it away!

Now write down positive phrases like these:

"I can do it ... "   *"Let's give it a try ... "*

"Why not?"   *"I think it'll work!"*

Add your own to this list — and post it somewhere in your room where you'll be sure to see it every day.

Another technique to try is called "self-talk" or "inner speech." Self-talk is anything you say to yourself, in your mind or out loud.

Think about the last time you forgot your homework at home. Or think about the last time you dropped something breakable on the floor. What did you say to yourself? Did you use words like "dumb," "failure," "lazy," "clumsy," "ugly," "klutzy," "stupid," "clod," "loser," "jerk," or "disorganized"? Eliminate them from your mental vocabulary — starting today.

It helps to have a "cheer-up" sentence in reserve for those times when you're *really* feeling down, depressed, defeated, or lonely. Here are a few examples to store in your mind:

"I'm healthy, strong, and comfortable."

"I'm good at _____, _____, and _____."

"The people who like me include _____, _____, and _____."

"The last really terrific thing I did was _____."

Remember: you are what you think you are.

THREE WAYS TO SHARPEN YOUR THINKING SKILLS

Thinking is something you're going to have to keep doing for the rest of your life. Here are a few ways to get better and better at it:

1) Learn to see the "big picture."

Some people can grasp bits and pieces of a situation but have a hard time viewing it as a whole. Seeing the "big picture" takes *strategic thinking*, and it's something you can practice.

Start by asking yourself this very simple question:

"What's going on?"

Then break this down by looking at specifics.

? Where are you? Scan your setting and note details.

? Who are you with? If there are other people present, pay attention to what they're doing.

? What's your relationship to those people? That may determine what you do next.

2) Learn to think on your feet.

There are people who are good at this. You know who they are: they're the ones who are always coming up with a snappy line or a solution to a problem in a split second.

◆ Start by closely observing your situation. Again: what's going on? Where are you? Who are you with? What are they doing? What's your relationship to them?

◆ Think about what *you* want. Set clear goals.

◆ Don't procrastinate; act! Maybe the decision you make won't be the best one possible. But at least you will have done something. And the better you get at thinking on your feet, the better your decisions will become.

3) Be flexible.

According to one study done at Colgate University, students who took math tests while lying on the floor with their feet slightly raised did better than students who sat upright at their desks. They completed the test 8% faster — and their answers were 14% more accurate.

Maybe your teacher won't let you do this. But it can't hurt to ask!

Here are some other ideas to consider:

▽ Do you always do your homework before dinner? Try doing it later for a week or so. You may notice an improvement.

○ Take notes on colored typing paper instead of lined white notebook sheets. The colors may inspire you.

□ The next time you start a new class, don't head for your "usual" spot. Sit in the front or the middle. Sit by the door instead of by the window.

> **"The world is a tragedy to those who feel, and a comedy to those who think."**
>
> — **William Shakespeare** *(English playwright, poet, and actor, author of at least 37 comedies, histories, and tragedies, and knowledgeable in subjects including music, law, science, stage art, and sports)*

The Art of Listening

When you're supposed to be listening, do things go in one ear and out the other? That's an entertaining image, but it doesn't describe what actually happens. All kinds of sounds — talking, music, traffic noises, airplanes flying overhead, birds chirping, floorboards squeaking — come into your head via your ears every day. And they don't exit out the other side. Instead, your brain chooses to use them or lose them.

You have a lot of control over what you listen to. One reason is because your brain processes information 4-10 times faster than the speed of speech. So even if you wanted to, you couldn't take it all in. But you can decide what to pay attention to and retain.

Remember the last time you sat through a particularly boring lecture? Did your mind tend to wander in a million different directions? Being a good listener involves more than keeping your ears open and your mouth closed. It's a perceptual skill that depends on your attitude at the time.

Are you willing to learn something new? Can you convince yourself to get interested? Are there advantages to listening closely to what's being said? Can this information help you to reach a particular goal?

Too many people have poor listening habits. They're so wrapped up in themselves and what they're going to say or do next that they neglect to listen. Or they're easily distracted. Or they seem to listen closely but immediately forget everything they hear.

Many businesses and companies are training their employees to be better listeners. Schools should be doing the same with their students. Most aren't, and that's too bad, because students spend 60-70% of their classroom time listening. Or, at least, that's what they're *supposed* to be doing.

What kind of listener are you? Here are some ways to improve your listening skills:

 The next time you end up in a boring situation (and you will), don't tune out. Tune in. Be "all ears" for a change and see what happens.

 Don't don't just sit there; *do something*. Take notes, placing special emphasis on key words or phrases. Make lists: of questions to ask afterward, of ideas to explore further on your own, of points you disagree with. Use these lists later on to refresh your memory.

If you want to know more about thinking, read:
** *Make the Most of Your Mind* by Tony Buzan (New York: Linder Press/Simon and Schuster, 1984).
*** *Brain Power* by Karl Albrecht (Englewood Cliffs, New Jersey: Prentice-Hall, Inc., 1980).

MEMORY AND LEARNING

You stroll into class and sit down at your desk. Then your teacher gives you your first assignment of the day:

"Memorize this list of numbers in less than one minute:"

1 5 1 8 5 9 3 7 6 5 5 0 2 1 5 7 8 4 1 6 6 5 9 5 0 6 1 1 2 9 0 4 8 5 6 8 6 7 7 2 7 3 1 4 1 8 1 8 6 1 0 5 4 6 2 9 7 4 8 0 1 2 9 4 9 7 4 9 6 5 9 2 8.

Sounds impossible, right? But a young university student from Pittsburgh named Dario Donetelli was able to repeat this list (in order, with no mistakes) only *48 seconds* after hearing it.

Another person with an awesome memory was the Russian journalist Solomon Shereshevskii, known as "S." Although he never took notes, he could repeat everything that was ever said to him, word for word. (If someone sneezed, S would have trouble recalling what was said because the sneeze was like a blur in his memory.) S had such remarkable imagery and memory capacity that he ended up being a stage performer. Unfortunately, he was *unable* to forget anything and ended up with too much information packed inside his head. He became easily confused and couldn't even hold a normal conversation.

Most people don't have memories like Dario or S, but our memories are amazing just the same. How many things do you remember in the course of a normal day? 50? 200? 5,000? 10,000? Maybe 50 seems too low and 10,000 too high. Surprise: you actually remember *billions* of things within each 24-hour period.

Within the three pounds of wrinkled flesh that make up your brain are telephone numbers, commercial jingles, the taste of yesterday's school lunch, faces of famous people, birthdays, the way a dog's coat feels, the smell of your grandma's perfume ... all the images, facts, and experiences of a lifetime.

Your memory plays an important role in *everything* you do. All learning depends on memory — and memory is far more than simply recalling a lot of facts. It also involves remembering thinking patterns. (Like the logical thinking patterns we talked about earlier.)

The memory is both powerful and mysterious. No two people remember exactly the same things in exactly the same ways, even if their lives are almost identical. No one knows exactly how memory works or why it fails us at times. That's because studying the memory is like trying to understand the workings of a complicated machine without being able to take it apart and look inside.

Memory seems to be located everywhere and nowhere in the brain. And your brain seems to have unlimited capacity for storing memories. If you took in 1,000 new bits of information every second from the day you were born until you were very old, you'd still have plenty of room left over.

Our brain takes in more information than we realize. Some experts think that it may actually remember *everything* we hear, taste, smell, touch, see, and experience. Others disagree. They claim that if this happened we'd be overloaded and maybe even schizophrenic.

Over 2,000 years ago, the Greek philosopher Aristotle suggested that the mind was "imprinted" with memories — like soft wax imprinted with a ring. Scientists today are discovering that he may have been right.

In 1969, a Canadian professor named Wilde Penfield conducted a series of experiments on the brains of some of his patients. When he stimulated certain parts with small electrical charges, the patients were able to visualize mental pictures from the past — including long-buried memories from childhood. They also got impressions of sounds, smells, colors, and tastes related to these past events. Penfield's experiments seem to indicate that memory "pathways" or "traces" do exist.

It would take another whole book to begin to explain the many theories about how the brain stores information. For now, let's leave it at this: Whenever your senses take in any kind of data, electrochemical circuits are formed between your neurons. These "connections" are what result in stored memories.

Six Types of Memory

Earlier we talked about the possibility that we might have many different intelligences. That issue is still open to question. Most scientists do agree, however, that we have several types of memory. Let's look at some of these.

1 **Short-Term Memory**, also called the "working memory," stores information that's needed for a brief period of time. It includes the ability to recall from six to eight different items within specific categories. Examples: your spelling words for this week, the melodies to popular songs, license plate numbers. When you "cram" for a test, you're using your short-term memory.

2 **Long-Term Memory** stores information over a long period of time so you can get it when you need it. **Examples:** your best friend's telephone number, your father's birthday, the meanings of words, a foreign language.

3 **Sensory Memory** is important to the way we perceive the world. It contains sensory impressions that we *never* forget, like the taste of peppermint candy, the sound of your favorite rock song, the smell of roses, andthe way a cat's fur feels. Almost *every* taste or smell you experience forms a permanent record in your brain.

4 **Motor Skill Memory** has to do with physical activities like riding a bicycle, throwing a ball, brushing your teeth, and swimming. These are things you learn by repetition, which makes them very hard to forget. (Practice doesn't just make perfect; it also makes permanent!)

> "I hear and I forget;
> I see and I remember;
> I do and I understand."
> — Old Oriental saying

5 **Verbal/Semantic Memory** enables you to know the meanings of words and math concepts. Most of us can remember several hundred thousand words and their meanings. In fact, some of the things we've talked about in this book have probably become part of your verbal and semantic memory.

6 **Photographic Memory** , also called "picture memory," stores images that remain as vivid as photographs in your mind. People who have a highly-developed form of this memory can remember whole pages of books, including punctuation marks. Unfortunately, photographic memory usually lasts for only a short period of time.

A sort of "subcategory" of this memory is called "eidetic memory," and it's fairly common in young children: about 20 in 500 have it. But it usually fades away before age 13. Maybe it's because our educational system stresses logic and language over imagination.

DÉJÀ VU: THE MIND'S TWILIGHT ZONE

Have you ever had the experience of being in an entirely new situation when suddenly you're *sure* you've lived through it before? Did it seem as if you *knew* your surroundings, the people around you, and the feelings you were having?

This eerie experience is known as *déjà vu*. Scientists think that it may be related to something called "memory units." These memory units might be so complete as to include vivid and accurate sensory pictures of a place, setting, or circumstance.

The psychologist Carl Jung believed that we all have a "memory storehouse" that we share with others at different times and places without even knowing it. He thought that people everywhere could tap into one another's "storehouses."

The next time you have that *déjà vu* feeling, think about this: Maybe those aren't your memories at all. Maybe they're someone else's!

Why We Forget

Now that we know something about how we remember, let's find out why we forget.

To begin with, nobody on earth has a "perfect" memory. Some people may have better memories than others, and some may have photographic memories, but they can't remember *everything* they experience during their lives. (Or, at least, they can't retrieve each and every one of those memories.)

Most of us forget more than 99% of the phone numbers we learn and more than 90% of the names of the people we meet. Pretty shabby!

We've all had the feeling that a particular memory was on the "tip of our tongue" — and no matter how hard we try, we haven't been able to get to it.

The reasons why people forget are almost as numerous as the ways in which they remember. Here are just a few:

Some people have cluttered minds, plain and simple. They need to do some "brain cleaning!"

But your brain doesn't have to be like a messy drawer, with socks and underwear falling out of it all the time. One way to avoid this is by assigning mental "labels" to new information coming in.

Some people forget things because they're poor listeners and don't pay attention. We've already talked about this. Another good way to sharpen your listening (and memory) skills is to softly repeat to yourself something you really want to remember.

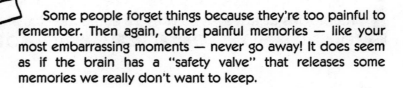
Some people forget things because they're too painful to remember. Then again, other painful memories — like your most embarrassing moments — never go away! It does seem as if the brain has a "safety valve" that releases some memories we really don't want to keep.

Other "memory blocks" — things that help you to *not* remember — include stress, mental strain, and fear. It's possible to break some of these down, but don't press too hard. Forcing yourself to remember something could backfire and result in your forgetting even more. This may explain "stage fright" and the horrible feeling of not remembering *anything* after overstudying for a test.

Improving Your Memory

The bad news is: there are some things you *will* forget. The good news is: you *can* improve your memory.

You could visit any library or bookstore and find tons of ideas for expanding your memory capacity. Some of them may be worth trying; others may be a big waste of time. Only you can decide what works for you.

The best approach to take is a very basic one: use your memory as often as possible! The more you use it, the better it will get.

We asked over 400 students to share with us their "tricks" for memorizing things. Here's a sampling of what they said:

◄ "Make up poems for them." Katy, 11

◄ "I try to make up a tune for it." Melodie, 11

◄ "Associate them with other things that I already know." Shawn, 14

◄ "If I have to memorize something, I'll memorize a word out of each sentence. That helps me with the whole thing." Cindy, 15

◄ "I use anagrams sometimes." Melissa, 15

◄ "I read them right before bed, or practice them a lot." Tony, 12

These are all *great* ideas. Maybe you've come up with some of your own. It doesn't matter what you do, as long as it does the job!

Most of us are taught to memorize things in school. (And a lot of us end up hating the things we have to memorize. Too often, they're poems — and that's why so many grownups don't like poetry. What a shame.) But we're not taught how to make the most of our memories. *Rote* memory — the kind that comes from repeating things over and over, often without paying any attention to what they mean — doesn't begin to tap our potential.

Here are a few more ideas for improving your memory:

If there's something you really want to remember, write it down. Then, even if you forget it, you'll be able to learn it again.

Keep a calendar handy. A pocket-sized one can be used for making notes and jotting down thoughts you have during the day.

Keep a notepad and pencil by your bed. Some of our greatest ideas occur to us just as we're dropping off to sleep.

If you're reading something you want to remember, read it aloud to yourself. You can improve your learning and memory by as much as 40% by using this simple tactic.

Don't stick to just one way of memorizing things. You may want to develop one approach for memorizing poems, and another for memorizing math formulas.

Interestingly, the time of day may affect how much you remember. Studies have shown that you remember more if you study right before you go to sleep. Also, people usually remember more of something if they learn it in the afternoon instead of the morning.

But *your* best time to learn can be *anytime*. Your brain is *always* taking in new information.

Mnemonics

Mnemonics — pronounced "nem-AH-niks" — are special memory "tricks" that can help you remember almost anything. Your teachers have probably already taught you some mnemonics. Here are two that we think are especially useful:

ACRONYMS

Acronyms are short phrases or initials which can help you remember a particular sequence of words. Some examples:

- Would you like to remember all the colors of the spectrum — the ones you see in the rainbow — in the correct order? Try "ROY G. BIV" — for **R**ed, **O**range, **Y**ellow, **G**reen, **B**lue, **I**ndigo, and **V**iolet.

- How about the Great Lakes? "HOMES" — for **H**uron, **O**ntario, **M**ichigan, **E**rie, and **S**uperior.

- Maybe you already know the nine planets, starting with the one closest to the sun. If not, this will help: "**M**y **V**ery **E**xcellent **M**om **J**ust **S**erved **U**s **N**ine **P**izzas." What it stands for, of course, is **M**ercury, **V**enus, **E**arth, **M**ars, **J**upiter, **S**aturn, **U**ranus, **N**eptune, and **P**luto.

Now create an acronym of your own for the parts of the brain we've talked about: the **b**rain **s**tem, the **c**erebellum, the **c**erebrum, and the **c**ortex.

B ___ S ___ C ___ C ___ C ___

THE LOCI TECHNIQUE

The LOCI technique has you visualize a "path" and specific "landmarks" along that path. When you want to remember something, you associate it with a landmark.

Let's say you wanted to remember a list of items to take on a camping trip.

You might start by assuming that the path will go through your house or apartment.

Now assign these landmarks:

1. Kitchen sink
2. Refrigerator
3. Cupboard
4. Stove
5. Medicine cabinet
6. Bathtub
7. Toilet
8. Bedroom closet
9. Dresser drawer
10. Bed

These are the ten items you need to remember to bring:

1. toothbrush
2. sleeping bag
3. lantern
4. pans
5. insect repellent
6. matches
7. underwear
8. marshmallows
9. guitar
10. crossword puzzle books

How can you match up the two lists? You might not be able to unless you let your imagination go. That's one of the fun parts of the LOCI technique: you can imagine almost anything, and it doesn't have to make sense!

For example:

VISUALIZE YOUR [toothbrush] FLOATING IN THE KITCHEN [sink]

WHAT COLOR IS IT? NOW IMAGINE THAT THE [refrigerator] DOOR

IS OPEN BECAUSE THE [bag] IS STICKING OUT OF IT.

NEXT YOU OPEN THE CUPBOARD [cupboard] AND SEE THE

LIT [lamp]. THEN YOU TOUCH THE HOT [stove] AND BURN

YOUR HAND ON THE [pan]. GO TO THE [cabinet] AND

GRAB THE LARGE CAN OF [insect off]. IN THE [bathtub] IS

A [tube]. TO YOUR SURPRISE, THE [toilet] IS CLOGGED

WITH YOUR [cup]. PROCEED TO YOUR BEDROOM

[window], OPEN THE DOOR AND THERE'S A GIANT

[marshmallow] WAITING TO GOBBLE YOU UP. INSIDE YOUR

[dresser] YOU FIND YOUR OLD [guitar] WITH ALL ITS [strings]

MISSING. FINALLY, YOU REACH YOUR [bed] AND FIND

A PILE OF [books] THAT YOUR SISTER HAS SCRIBBLED IN.

91

You can use the LOCI technique with almost any location and item. The wildest images are often the most powerful ones, and they tend to stick with you longer. When you use the LOCI technique, try to include these:

 ■ **extra bright colors**

■ **rhythm**

■ **silly or absurd connections**

■ **movement**

■ **sense of touch, taste, smell, and hearing, as well as seeing**

■ **exaggeration**

■ **humor**

If you want to find out more about memory and learning, read:

* *Improve Your Memory Skills* by Francis S. Bellezzy (Englewood Cliffs, New Jersey: Prentice-Hall, Inc., 1982).
* *How To Improve Your Memory* by Dan Halacy (New York: Franklin Watts, 1977).
*** *Your Memory: A User's Guide* by Alan Baddeley (Middlesex, England: Penguin Books, 1982).

CREATIVITY

It's no accident that many incredible discoveries have been made by people in their teens and early 20s. Galileo made his first important scientific observation at age 17. Handel composed music at age 11. Carl Gauss, a famous mathematician, was doing research at age 15.

This is not to say that your creativity will decline as you get older. But right now, at this moment, your young and relatively uncluttered brain has more room than it will ever have for new and brilliant ideas. So you may be in the prime of your life for enhancing your creativity!

Everyone exercises his or her creativity in unique and personal ways. As you come up with novel ways to comb your hair, fix your breakfast, set the table, do your homework, write a story, or arrange your room, you're being creative. How you walk, dress, talk, and act also demonstrate your creativity.

Most experts agree: *every* person is creative. In other words, creativity isn't something you either have or don't have. It's more a matter of degree than ability. Some people are creative in a big way; others are more subtle.

Creativity is both hard to define and difficult to measure. (It's a lot like intelligence.) By the way, there are no proven connections between creativity and I.Q. Just because a person is a "genius" doesn't necessarily mean that he or she is creative. On the other hand, a person who thinks creatively isn't necessarily tops on the intelligence scale.

Your creativity depends on what *you* do with the knowledge in *your* head.

■■

"Our rewards come not from having brains, but in using them."

— **Gerard I. Nierenberg** (author of The Art of Creative Thinking)

■■

How do creative people come up with their ideas? Sometimes in idiosyncratic ways. Many creative people have been considered eccentric — even weird.

■ When he was a young man, Beethoven often poured cold water over his head because he thought it would stimulate his brain.

■ Whenever he sat down to write, Charles Dickens would turn his head to the north because he thought the magnetic forces of the Pole would help him to create.

■ Rudyard Kipling would only use black ink to write with.

■ Johann Schiller, a German poet and playwright, was stimulated by the odor of decomposing apples, so he always kept some on his desk.

You probably have a few strange habits of your own. Whenever you're getting ready to create something, what do you do? Sit in a special chair? Wear a particular item of clothing? Rub your rabbit's foot?

Describing certain people as "creative" can be misleading. Instead, it's more accurate to say that they *think* creatively. This implies that they produce ideas when they use their brains in a certain way.

94

Creative thinking leads to creative results. When you're thinking creatively, you're searching for ideas and *using* your knowledge and experience to go off in new directions. Knowledge is essential to creative thinking. In fact, every new idea is a combination of two or more *known* ideas.

Creativity doesn't spring up by accident. It's a mental process, and like any other mental process it takes practice to get good at it. An open mind and a sense of humor can help. So can going beyond the expected and seeking out unexplored possibilities.

A large part of this mental process involves making connections and linking ideas together for the fun of it. Several inventive people have become famous for doing this well. **For example:**

In 1948 George de Mestral, a Swiss engineer, was climbing in the Alps when he noticed that burrs were sticking to his clothing. As he pulled them off, he saw how the tiny hooks on each burr clung to the thread loops on the fabric. He decided to invent a fastener that would stick like a burr. It took him eight years, but he finally did it. Today his invention — we know it as Velcro — is used in jackets, tennis shoes, spacesuits, and artificial hearts.

Noah Bucher of St. Paul, Minnesota was only 9 years old when he invented a new kind of underwear. While folding the laundry, he noticed a hole in a pair of his long johns. Instead of mending the hole, he tore it some more. Then he pulled the ripped long johns over his head upside-down, stuck his arms through the legs, and went to show his mom. Today Noah's colorful "Topp Drawers" are sold in stores across the nation.

These are only two examples of people who have used their creative thinking skills to come up with extraordinary ideas. There have been — and will be — thousands more. Maybe you'll be one!

THE FOUR STAGES
OF CREATIVE THINKING

Although there's no single fail-safe method for improving creativity, there are some creative processes that seem to work better than others. One that's especially highly regarded was devised by G. Wallas in 1926.

According to Wallas, creative thinking occurs in four major stages:

Preparation involves collecting knowledge and information as background for the problem under consideration. (Michelangelo first had to learn human anatomy before creating his sculptures.)

Incubation involves resting and relaxing to allow images from the unconscious to surface. During this "sitting and thinking" time, the creative thinker begins visualizing parts of the idea or solution. (Einstein once told a friend that he got some of his best ideas while shaving.)

Illumination comes suddenly and unexpectedly: the idea or solution just pops into your brain. The lightbulb goes off over your head and you experience an "Aha!" (Isaac Newton got his first insight into gravity while sitting in an apple orchard and watching an apple fall from a tree.)

Verification involves testing, proving, and carrying out an idea or solution to see if it really works. (The Wright Brothers tested their biplane by keeping it in the air for 12 seconds. This was long enough to prove that a heavy machine could fly — with people in it.)

Do You Have a Creative Attitude?

When you consider both famous and not-so-famous creative thinkers (like the wild and crazy guy who sits next to you in study period), you probably recognize some common traits. An especially obvious one is their *creative attitude.*

Whether they "look" creative on the outside isn't important. Some creative thinkers are creative dressers; others could care less what they wear, as long as they don't get arrested. It's what goes on *inside* their heads that counts.

How many of these characteristics do you share?

- **Creative thinkers dare to be different.** They're true risk-takers who not only accept but thrive on uncertainty. They prefer working on the edge to working at the center.

- **Creative thinkers are self-motivated and have a positive self-image.** They meet challenges optimistically and feel good about themselves and their accomplishments. They ignore people who tell them, "It'll never work!" Peer pressure and group pressure don't faze them in the least.

- **Creative people enjoy working on problems — the harder, the better.** They're happiest when facing complex problems and searching for many alternative solutions. They consider many possibilities and outcomes. They may become totally absorbed in their task — ignoring the time, skipping meals, and forgetting to sleep while they're working.

Think about some of the creative thinkers you know. How are they different from most other people?

 — Albert Einstein

Invisible Fences

Not everyone finds it easy to open up and think creatively. Sometimes "invisible fences" — mental blocks — get in the way.

Here are some of the most common invisible fences: being afraid to make a mistake; being afraid of criticism; being afraid of being laughed at; and being afraid of losing friends.

How are these alike? They all involve fear of some kind. These fears are natural and may never disappear completely. But positive thinking can help you overcome them. (To refresh your mind about positive thinking, turn back to page 75.)

For example: Instead of thinking "I don't want to make a mistake," think "A mistake may teach me something." Instead of thinking, "I hope no one criticizes me," think "I will try to accept criticism and learn from it." And so on.

Some invisible fences are the result of pattern thinking. While pattern thinking can be beneficial, getting in a rut can slow you down.

The mind tends to focus on tried-and-true patterns — they're comfortable and don't require any effort to understand. But breaking a pattern can stretch creativity (and lead to solutions that formerly seemed impossible).

For example: Take a look at this dot pattern. Now, without lifting your pencil from the paper or doing any retracing, draw 4 straight lines that pass through all 9 dots.

●   ●   ●

●   ●   ●

●   ●   ●

Most people can't solve this problem because when they look at the dots they see a square — a square that isn't really there. The sides of the nonexistent square pen them in.

If you can't connect the dots, try thinking of them in this way: They're floating in a two-dimensional space. There are no top, bottom, or side boundaries.

Does this make a difference?

If you still can't connect the dots, turn to page 106 for the answer.

Another invisible fence that gets in the way of creative thinking is the "one-right-answer" attitude. We're all taught this in school to some degree. Multiple-choice tests allow for one right answer. Teachers ask oral questions and expect one right answer.

Where would we be today if the great inventors of the world had all been searching for one right answer? In reality, there often are *many* solutions to the same problem.

A lot of schools place too much emphasis on *convergent thinking* — pulling facts together to find (again) one right answer. You use convergent thinking to answer questions like these:

▶ What is the capital of Minnesota?

▶ Who wrote the national anthem?

▶ How many pints are in a gallon?

▶ Who invented the cotton gin?

The opposite of convergent thinking is *divergent thinking*, which permits several possible answers. Divergent thinking is creative, imaginative thinking. There are no "wrong" answers. You use divergent thinking to solve problems like these:

● How many uses can you think of for a wooden spoon?

● Look at these 12 squares. What can you do with them?

☐ ☐ ☐ ☐

☐ ☐ ☐ ☐

☐ ☐ ☐ ☐

Convergent thinking isn't necessarily "bad," and divergent thinking isn't necessarily "good." Actually, creative thinkers use *both* kinds to solve problems and generate new ideas. Divergent thinking lets the ideas come; convergent thinking verifies them.

Enhancing Your Creativity

Some people seem to think creatively with almost no effort. In fact, creative thinking takes hard work and commitment. But, as any creative thinker will tell you, it can also be a lot of fun!

There's no magic formula for enhancing creativity. Since it doesn't appear to be controllable, maybe it *can't* be enhanced. (Scratch that negative thought!) Still, studies seem to indicate that people can become more creative if they put their minds to it.

One of the first people to suggest that creativity is part of the intellect was J.P. Guilford. He was interested in learning how creativity develops, so he studied the divergent thinking process. What he found was a way to describe creative thinking in terms of four creative "products": fluency, flexibility, originality, and elaboration.

Fluency leads to the generation of a large number of ideas. Brainstorming — and making lists of brainstormed idea — is one way to enhance it. **Example:** List as many uses as you can for a soda straw.

Flexibility requires a variety of thought categories and the ability to shift from one to another to generate more ideas. Example: Use the word "light" — and its different meanings — to come up with as many sentences as you can.

Originality leads to clever and unique ideas. (Originality is difficult to define because everyone has his or her own opinion of what it means.) It's not very common, and often it seems like the result of pure chance or luck. Example: Think of how the world would be different if people had two heads OR if grass was pink instead of green.

Elaboration is the process of building on ideas or solutions by expanding them, adding details, and refining them. **Example:** How could you combine a can opener and a calculator to produce a new invention? What would it do?

Chances are, you've already done exercises like these in school. That's terrific! Keep practicing creative thinking, and you're bound to become more fluent, flexible, original, and elaborate.

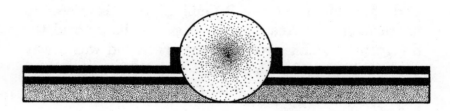

TWENTY WAYS TO BECOME MORE CREATIVE THAN YOU ALREADY ARE

1) Spend time with creative people.

2) Write down your ideas so you can't lose them.

3) Laugh! Enhance your sense of humor, too. Read cartoon books. Watch comedy programs. Tell jokes with your friends. Ask somebody to tickle you.

4) Assume that anything is possible. Fantasize.

5) List everything positive about yourself that you can think of. **For example:** "I get along well with other people."

6) Ask "What If" questions — the crazier, the better. (What if the sky was red? What if people had only one eye, like the Cyclops? What if ants were larger than humans? What if lakes were made of chocolate?)

7) Make up similes, metaphors, and analogies. Use these as jumping-off places. (A brain is like a bank — you can only take out as much as you put in. Riding a bike is like . Taking a test is like.)

8) Design new inventions to solve messy problems.

9) Play "Just Suppose." (Just suppose I decided to run for class president . . . Just suppose I came up with a new way to clean the birdcage . . . Just suppose .)

10) Pay attention to "small" ideas. That's where many big ones get their start.

11) Look for different ways to express your creativity. Try painting, cooking, photography, writing, playing tennis, inventing, graffiti, etc.

12) Daydream. Let your mind wander.

13) If you're right-handed, try using your left hand to do things. If you're left-handed, switch to your right for a while.

14) Play strategy games like chess, backgammon, or bridge.

15) Stand on your head to get the blood really flowing to your brain.

16) Estimate and guess at measurements rather than using a yardstick, a tape measure, or a measuring cup.

17) Do your math homework *without* a calculator.

18) Read the first half of a novel and then stop. Write a juicy ending of your own.

19) Make lists. Then make more lists. (List as many words as you can think of that end in "-ment." List all the dogs you know by name.)

20) Imagine that your brain is like a locked door — and only you hold the key. Now put the key in the lock, turn it, and . . . .

SCAMPER: A Creative Thinking Checklist

Another way to enhance your creativity is by using a checklist called SCAMPER.

SCAMPER is an acronym for a series of thinking processes. It was developed by Bob Eberle, a well-known author of activity books for gifted kids. He based his idea on an earlier checklist from a book by Alex Osborn called *Applied Imagination: Principles and Procedures of Creative Problem Solving.* (See how one idea can lead to another?)

When you use the SCAMPER checklist, you start off with a particular object in mind and think about ways to change it. Here's what the acronym stands for:

S **Substitute:** What could be used instead?

C **Combine:** What could be added?

A **Adapt:** How can it be adjusted to suit a condition or purpose?

M **Modify:** How can the color, shape, or form be changed?

Magnify: How can it be made larger, stronger, or thicker?

Minify: How can it be made smaller, lighter, or shorter?

P **Put to other uses:** What else can it be used for?

E **Eliminate:** What can be removed or taken away from it?

R **Reverse:** How can it be turned around or placed opposite its original position?

Rearrange: How can the pattern, sequence, or layout be changed?

EXAMPLE: Imagine that the object you're thinking of is an umbrella. Here are some ways to SCAMPER it.

Substitute: Use a wire coat hanger and plastic wrap or a plastic bag.

Combine: Add a digital clock and radio inside the umbrella handle.

Adapt: Modify it for joggers who run in the rain. Make it lightweight, glow-in-the-dark, and easy to attach around the whole body.

Modify: Make it out of a material that dries instantly.

Magnify: Make it wide enough to keep two adults dry — or deep enough to cover a person to his or her knees.

Minify: Make it lighter — use a styrofoam handle? Or make it small enough to fold up and fit inside a purse.

Put to other uses: Dig holes with it.

Eliminate: Take away the handle; attach the umbrella instead to a headband, or prop it on a chair and use it as a sunshade.

Reverse: Turn it upside-down, hang it on a tree, and fill it with birdseed.

Rearrange: Put the handle on the side.

"The human mind, once stretched to a new idea, never goes back to its original dimensions."

— Oliver Wendell Holmes (*physician, educator, author, and poet*)

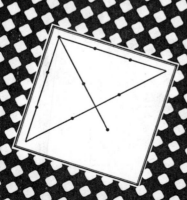

TLC F♥R Y♥UR BRAIN

Think of the many things you take care of: your pet, bike, clothes, books, souvenirs, stuffed animals, baseball cards, collections, photographs, teeth, bedroom, stereo, records and tapes . . . . We take care of things so they'll stay in good shape and last longer.

Because your brain is something you can't see or touch, it's easy to forget that it needs the same TLC (Tender Loving Care) that you give to your other valuable possessions. (Also, you've had it forever, so you probably take it for granted.)

In fact, it needs extra special attention from you, because once it's damaged it can't be fixed. It's not like a flat tire or a chipped tooth. The number of brain cells you have now is the same number you were born with; you can't grow any more. So the trick is to keep the cells you have in tip-top condition.

How? By giving your brain regular workouts. You've heard the old saying "use it or lose it." The more you use your brain, the less brain power you'll lose as you get older.

Actually, your intelligence can keep on growing well into your old age. Remember that learning creates new links between the neurons in your brain. If you never stop learning, your brain will continue forming those important new connections.

The acronym RED can help you remember to take care of your brain. It stands for **Rest, Exercise, and Diet.**

Rest: Give Your Brain a Break

Rest is essential to both your body *and* your brain.

Your body runs on a daily "action or rest" cycle. It uses the time when you're asleep to replace old cells with new ones. A disruption to the cycle can interfere with this growth process.

It can also affect your brain's rhythms. Like your body, your brain uses your "down time" to replenish itself. While you dream, your brain is generating chemicals and proteins you used up while you were awake.

You should also take study breaks and rest during the day. Your brain is under a lot of stress! Kids today are exposed to louder noises and more stimuli than ever. Rock music, traffic, airplanes, telephones ringing, TVs blaring — they all add up. Processing these stimuli takes a massive mental effort. (Did you know that the average child watches 25,000 TV commercials per year?) That's why it's important to spend some time each day doing nothing. Kick back, close your eyes, and shut out the world. Give your overworked brain the chance to slow down.

One good way to do this is by meditating. Some people choose to learn this skill by studying TM (Transcendental Meditation) or taking classes in other forms of meditation. But you can also teach yourself the basics. Try this:

1 Find a comfortable, quiet place to sit down — an overstuffed chair, or your bed (with pillows at your back).

2 Close your eyes and take several slow, deep breaths. Establish this as your "breathing pattern" during your meditation session.

3 Focus on relaxing every part of your body — starting with your feet and working up. (You may even want to say to yourself, "Feet, relax . . . Ankles, relax . . . Calves, relax . . . Knees, relax . . . Thighs, relax . . . ," and so on.) By the time you get to "Head, relax," you should feel a release of tension.

4 If you like, make up your own "mantra." A mantra is a word or phrase you repeat over and over in your mind. It can be anything — nonsense syllables, your own name, a word like "umbrella." In do-it-yourself meditation, the point of a mantra is to block out both your "inner voice" and outside noises.

5 Keep breathing deeply and saying your mantra (if you're using one) for a period of time that feels right to you — ten minutes, fifteen minutes, half an hour. (You may get so laid-back that you fall asleep!)

Most people who meditate claim that it not only relaxes them but fills them with energy. Calming your mind can also increase your memory capacity, problem-solving abilities, and creativity.

You may want to schedule a regular time each day for your meditation. Or take a "meditation break" whenever you're feeling extra stressed — like during exam time.

Exercise: Get Moving!

Regular physical exercise can boost your brain power. (One study of schoolchildren in Canada showed that kids who exercised daily got higher grades.) Exercise can also increase your imagination and make you feel better about yourself. If you don't believe this, ask a jogger!

Exercise not only burns fat and gets your body into shape, it also helps your heart and lungs to function better and last longer.

● **Aerobic exercise** is essential to your cardiorespiratory system (that's your heart and lungs). Examples: jogging, walking (at a clip, *not* a stroll), swimming, bicycling, the aerobics class at your local Y.

● **Stretching and repetition exercises** are important to your flexibility and muscle tone. Examples: yoga, pushups and situps, Nautilus exercises, weight-lifting.

What's the best way to form the exercise habit? By starting *today* (not tomorrow). Make up a regular exercise plan for the week and follow it faithfully. In almost no time you'll feel more alert, energetic, and with-it.

Diet: Food for Thought

What goes into your body through your mouth can directly affect your thinking. Unfortunately, eating a well-balanced diet isn't easy for kids on the go.

Scientists are learning more and more about the relationship between food and the brain. Here are some general guidelines:

■ Stick to fresh, natural foods: fruits, vegetables, grains, beans, leafy greens. They contain vitamins which help you to breathe better and increase your alertness.

■ Avoid foods that have been "tampered with" — those that contain added sugars, starches, and artificial preservatives.

■ Say NO to caffeine (found in many carbonated drinks), alcohol, and drugs. These may make you feel more "awake" for a while, but it's just an illusion. Too much can actually lead to mental dullness (and worse).

Anything you eat will eventually "go to your head."
To improve your thinking, think before you eat!

BIOFEEDBACK

A famous Tibetan yogi could sit in the snow and generate enough body heat to melt a circle around himself.

A person in an experiment raised the temperature in his right hand by visualizing himself touching a hot stove — and, at the same time, *lowered* the temperature in his left hand by visualizing himself squeezing an ice cube.

What did they have that you don't have? Special abilities? Supernatural powers? Bionic implants?

No — all they had was *knowledge* of how their bodies work. Almost anyone with that knowledge can learn to control certain bodily functions. If you wanted to, you could probably learn how to lower your blood pressure, change your body temperature, reduce your heart rate, or alter your brain waves.

Biofeedback is one way to find out about what's going on inside your body. The definition of *feedback* is "information returned to itself." Biofeedback involves hooking yourself up to a biofeedback machine — a type of electronic equipment — that translates your bodily functions into sounds or signals. For example, a certain sound from the machine might indicate that your heart is beating too fast, or a light might show what kinds of brainwaves you're producing.

Dr. Barbara Brown, a brain researcher, designed a unique and exciting experiment involving biofeedback. The test subjects — children — wore electrodes on their heads that led to a brain wave monitor, and the monitor in turn was connected to an electric train set. Whenever the children's brains produced alpha waves, the train moved! Experiments like these demonstrate the partnership between mind and body.

Biofeedback is sometimes used in treating illnesses. It's been estimated that 75% of all illnesses are related to stress. Ulcers, headaches, sore throats, and even heart attacks have been traced back to stress. Using biofeedback, people can learn to quiet their minds and alleviate their stress-related aches and pains.

Although biofeedback offers new possibilities for self-improvement and body control, it hasn't yet established itself as a science. Some experts have written it off as a fad; others believe that its benefits have been exaggerated. Still others point out that inadequate equipment and stray signals can affect the biofeedback process and lead to wrong conclusions. Even so, many hospitals and universities use biofeedback in treating patients and doing research.

The jury is still out on whether biofeedback is a valid tool, but it does seem to have many potential uses. For now, we know that it can measure what's happening inside us, and that takes us one step closer to understanding.

HYPNOSIS AND SELF-HYPNOSIS

Can a stranger run up to you on the street, hypnotize you, and force you to rob a bank? Of course not! Still, hypnosis has gotten a bad name in some circles — mostly because people don't understand it.

If used correctly, hypnosis can help people overcome problems — like phobias and bad habits including nail-biting and smoking. It's been effectively used in medicine in a number of ways. Hypnotized women have delivered babies by Caesarian section without an anesthetic. Hypnotized people have gone through dental surgery without drugs.

When you're hypnotized, you enter an altered state of consciousness. You may seem to be asleep, or you may seem to be wide-awake and alert. There many different levels of hypnotic "sleep."

Most people can be hypnotized; in fact, about 90% of young people can be put into a very deep trance. But they can't be hypnotized without their consent. In fact, hypnosis won't "take" if you don't trust the hypnotist and aren't willing to cooperate.

Trained hypnotists use several methods to put people into trances. They may persuade their subjects to relax and block out distracting thoughts. Or they may ask them to feel their arms, legs, and eyelids getting heavy. Or they may use something called "sensory monotony" — having people stare at an object for a period of time. Or they may use visualization or imagery.

Hypnotized people have performed amazing feats, from lifting large, heavy objects to painting beautiful pictures. It's likely that the physical and mental capabilities needed to perform those feats were already there, and that hypnotism merely released them.

One characteristic common to all forms of hypnosis is a "directed link" between one level of consciousness and another. Hypnosis moves you out of the level you're at to another level you may not be able to get to on your own. Psychologists believe that there may be as many as 20 different states of consciousness.

Hypnosis can have positive results, but there are still unanswered questions — and genuine concerns — about its use. Nobody quite understands what happens when a person is hypnotized. Maybe someday someone will invent a way to measure brainwaves, pulse rates, skin responses, and eye movements of people in a trance; until then, hypnosis will probably remain a mystery.

Hypnosis isn't for amateurs, and it doesn't work for everyone. Inducing a trance may seem simple, but getting someone out of a trance can be difficult. Some people have stayed in a trance long after being hypnotized. Others have suffered emotional aftereffects. That's why *only qualified and trained professionals should perform hypnosis.* It's not a party game!

Serious hypnosis isn't something you should play with. But you can practice a mild form of *self-hypnosis* to help you relax and get in touch with your inner feelings.

Self-hypnosis is a safe and effective means of finding out more about yourself. If there's a particular goal you want to achieve, or if you want to improve yourself in some way, it's worth a try.

Hypnosis consultant Frank Shams recommends this technique for beginning your self-hypnosis routine:

1) Find a quiet room and a comfortable place to sit.

2) Close your eyes and mentally count backwards *slowly* from 50 to 0.

When you reach 0, you'll probably be in a light hypnotic state. (Even if you're not, you'll be more relaxed than you were when you started. This exercise is also a great tension reliever.)

What can you do with your newfound ability? You might want to use it to solve a problem you've been having. For example, let's say you're a nail-biter. You've made several attempts to quit, but you haven't had any success. So this is what you can do:

1) On a 3 × 5" card, write, "I want to stop biting my nails."

2) Read the card silently three times.

3) Now go into your light hypnotic state.

4) Once you're there, visualize yourself as a person who isn't a nail-biter. Talk to yourself softly but firmly.

5) When you feel that this message has gotten through to your subconscious, stop.

6) Gradually come out of your hypnotic state. You may want to take a few deep breaths and do a few stretches.

Whenever you're able to visualize a goal and mentally act it out, you have a greater chance of success. Naturally it's important to choose a *realistic* goal. No matter how many times you repeat to yourself, "I want to sprout wings and fly," it's not going to happen!

SLEEP AND DREAMS

In 1968, Mrs. Bertha Van Der Merwe of Capetown, South Africa went without sleep for 11 days, 18 hours, and 55 minutes. She set the world's record.

In 1959, a New York disk jockey named Peter Tripp stayed awake for 200 hours (that's more than 8 days) as a publicity stunt to raise money for charity.

For most people, these kinds of sleepless marathons are nearly impossible. Forty-eight hours are usually enough to make us feel weird and act strange. (Tripp had wild hallucinations. He thought he saw a friend's face on a clock dial, a fire in his dresser drawer, and a suit growing fuzzy worms!)

People who are deprived of sleep become grouchy, confused, and accident-prone and have a tough time doing their jobs or schoolwork. We *need* sleep.

But why?

One reason is because the human body operates on a 24-hour cycle. Our "body clock" functions according to Circadian rhythms — rhythms that correspond to certain hours of the day.

Every person's body clock is unique. Most people need about 8 hours of sleep per day and spend the other 16 on waking activities. Others seem to require less sleep (as little as 4-5 hours) or more (as much as 10 hours).

Another reason is that your body uses the hours when you're sleeping to make internal repairs. Still another reason may be due to "genetic programming."

Our long-ago ancestors slept when it was dark because it was too dangerous to hunt; maybe our DNA remembers.

Scientists don't know precisely why we need sleep. But they have a pretty good idea of what happens when we do drop off.

The Four Stages of Sleep

People used to believe that not much went on in the brain during sleep. Wrong! While you're out cold, parts of your brain are wide awake.

Researchers in sleep labs study sleeping people to learn what happens in both the mind and the body. They use several special instruments, the most common being the electroencephalograph, or EEG. Being hooked up to an EEG is a painless procedure: electrodes are taped to parts of the body. Wires run from the electrodes into the EEG and carry messages to it. The EEG records these messages as lines on a long roll of paper. A readout from a single night might be as much as 1,500 feet long!

The EEG tells the researchers about the four stages of sleep. Your brain travels back and forth between these stages all night long.

▶ **Stage I: Drifting off to sleep.** During this stage, your muscles relax, your body temperature drops, and your heart slows down. You may squirm around and change positions. (In a single night, you may change positions as often as 30 times.)

▶ **Stage II: Light sleep.** During this stage, you may keep squirming around. Since you're not yet "sound asleep," you may be easily awakened.

▶ **Stage III: Deep sleep.** During this stage, your blood pressure drops. You're not as easily awakened.

▶ **Stage IV: Deepest sleep.** During this stage, you may talk in your sleep or even walk in your sleep. It's very difficult to wake you up.

You stay in Stage IV for a few minutes, then move back through stages III and II and finally to Stage I.

This is the point at which you start to dream. After dreaming for about 20 minutes, you go back down through stages II, III, and IV. This up-down, yo-yo pattern continues throughout the night. As morning approaches, your dreams last longer and your deep-sleep stages are shorter.

Sleepwalking and Sleeptalking

Have you ever walked in your sleep? If you have, you probably don't remember anything that happened. Most sleepwalkers don't.

But at least you're not alone. About 4 million Americans are sleepwalkers. Some of them do amazing things.

- One college student had a habit of climbing out of bed in the middle of the night, getting dressed, walking a mile to a river, and going for a swim. Then he went back to his room and back to bed.

- Another person walked along a 12th-story ledge and never woke up (good thing!).

In each case, none of the sleepwalkers remembered what they had done. But all had a seemingly irresistible urge to do something specific. That's one characteristic all sleepwalkers share.

Why do some people sleepwalk? Once again, nobody knows for sure. Some experts think it may be hereditary. They do know that it has nothing to do with dreaming. In fact, sleepwalking occurs during the dreamless stages.

Sleeptalking has two things in common with sleepwalking: it takes place during the deeper stages of sleep, and the people who do it don't remember anything about it.

121

SLEEPLEARNING: FACT OR FICTION?

Wouldn't it be great if you could learn in your sleep? You could learn new things you don't have time for now. Or you could pack all those boring lectures into the middle of the night and save your daylight hours for more interesting pursuits.

A nice idea, but no go. At least, not yet.

Scientists have played tape-recorded lessons to sleeping test subjects. Companies have promoted taped foreign language, personality improvement, and stop-biting-your-nails programs. Unfortunately, there's no solid proof that sleep learning works. Apparently it's effective only during Stage I sleep.

But you're not in Stage I for very long at any given time, and it seems that your brain doesn't pay attention to recorded information during the other stages. Now, if someone would invent a machine that turned itself on and off *between* stages . . .

Dreams and Nightmares

Dreaming sleep is much more interesting than regular sleep. Scientists who study sleep have learned that dreamers' eyes move back and forth as if they're watching an exciting movie. This phenomenon is called Rapid Eye Movement, or REM.

When you're in REM sleep your heart beats faster and your breathing is heavier than usual. If you're awakened in the middle of it, you'll almost certainly be able to remember what you were dreaming.

- About one-third of dreams take place in houses; one-fourth are set in buses, cars, boats, trains, and other moving vehicles.

- People dream in color but usually remember their dreams in black-and-white.

- 40% of dreams are about strangers — people unknown to the dreamers.

Most dreams occur in familiar settings and involve events that happened during the daylight (or waking) hours. We dream about food, friends and family members, teachers, romance, problems, sporting events, tests, conversations, abstract ideas — anything and everything. Usually we don't have any control over what goes on in our dreams (but some people claim that they do).

Contemporary dream experts say that our dreams speak to us in symbols, paradoxes, and riddles. Psychiatrists and psychologists sometimes try to help people interpret their dreams and uncover their meanings.

REM sleep occurs approximately every 90 minutes. You spend a total of about 2 hours a night in this dreaming, "active" sleep state. If you miss out on it one night, your brain will "catch up" on the next.

Maybe you never remember your dreams. This doesn't mean that you don't dream, period. *Everyone* dreams. So do dogs, cats, and other mammals. (You've probably seen your dog "chasing cats" in its sleep. Its paws may twitch, and it may even growl or bark.)

Over your lifetime, you'll spend a total of from 4-6 years just dreaming. Here are some other interesting facts about dreaming:

Early in this century, Dr. Sigmund Freud suggested that dreams function like "guardians" of the mind, keeping forbidden thoughts tucked away in the unconscious. (The unconscious is where all of our memories and experiences are stored.) Freud also came up with the theory of "wish-fulfillment" dreams — dreams that express our deepest desires. (You're the star quarterback for the New York Jets ... you're an opera singer ... you're an astronaut.)

But maybe dreams don't have "hidden" meanings. Carl Jung, who started out as a friend and follower of Freud, later disagreed with Freud's theories and devised his own. He coined the term "collective unconscious" to refer to the vast array of human history that he believed was tucked away in everyone's unconscious. He saw the unconscious as the mind's director and advisor and believed that dreams can help us learn about our innermost thoughts and feelings.

Dreams may be a way of reviewing what happens in our lives and sorting out the things we don't understand. They do seem to mirror our emotions; if we're upset, angry, frustrated, happy, or scared during the day, these same feelings might surface in the dreams we have at night.

Dreams are usually enjoyable and entertaining. We may fly, or save the world, or ace a biology test, or win the heart of someone we have a crush on. But what about those times when our dreams *aren't* so pleasant?

When you wake up with your heart in your mouth, a sweaty body, and a racing pulse, you know you've had a nightmare! Here's the good news: nightmares are necessary and normal. Necessary because they act as a sort of "safety valve," giving you the opportunity to get in touch with your fears without actually putting yourself in danger. Normal because everybody has them.

Some dream experts think that people dream about ghosts, monsters, giant fanged animals, and slimy creatures when there's a disturbance in their life. Contrary to popular belief, eating certain foods before going to bed won't give you nightmares (although a spicy enchilada at midnight could keep you awake for awhile). So the next time you have one, don't blame it on the pickles!

Can you remember your worst nightmare? We asked some students to share theirs:

"When I was very small, I dreamed that my family had company and nobody was paying any attention to me. I went to get a glass of water and got pulled into the drain — and they never missed me."

"Once I dreamed I was reading a book when pirates came to my house and invited me to dinner. Then they ate me."

"I dreamed I was in a jail that was in our school. The teacher I liked the least was the one who was putting people in the jail. I got put in and had to stay there for two years. This was revealing because I hated that school and had two years left to go!"

Making Your Dreams Work for You

Are dreams just wasted time? Or can you *do* something with all the action that goes on in your head while you sleep?

● Some mathematicians claim that they have written complex equations in their sleep.

- Jack Nicklaus, a famous professional golfer, improved his golf score by practicing the way he dreamed he held his club.

- Robert Louis Stevenson based *The Strange Case of Dr. Jekyll and Mr. Hyde* on his nightmares.

- Freidrich August Kekule von Stradonitz, a German chemist, was trying to understand how carbon atoms are arranged in a molecule of a chemical called *benzene*. One day he took a nap and dreamed about six snakes biting one anothers' tails and whirling in circles. When he woke up, he understood the structure of the benzene ring.

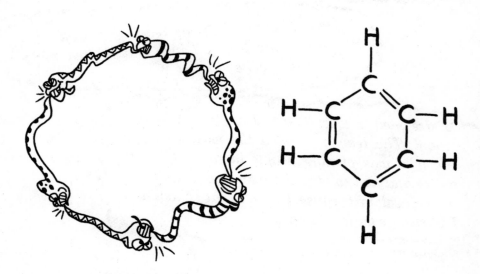

In order to use your dreams, you have to be able to remember them — and this isn't always easy. People who insist that they never dream only think that because they never remember their dreams.

Maybe you recall some and not others. If you'd like to hold on to more, try this approach:

1 Put a notebook, pen and paper, or tape recorder next to your bed. This will be your dream journal.

2 Just before going to sleep, "remind" yourself to dream. One way to do this is by visualizing something you want to dream about.

3 When you wake up, don't jump out of bed immediately. Instead, lie still for a few moments. The details of your dream may come back to you.

4 In your dream journal, record as much of your dream as you can recall. Do it immediately. A dream that isn't captured quickly tends to fade away and vanish.

Some people who *really* want to remember their dreams set their alarm clocks to go off in the middle of the night. Being awakened suddenly, and at a time when you're not usually awakened, can take a dream by surprise.

You may want to keep your dream journal with you during the day. A word, a gesture, or a situation may bring a dream rushing back into your consciousness.

Be sure to date the entries in your dream journal. Later you can look back to see how your dreams have related to the events in your life. Maybe you'll find patterns, or dream series, or recurrent dreams — dreams that happen over and over again. Their meanings may not seem clear at first, but sooner or later you'll probably make discoveries about yourself.

★ ✦ ✦ ✦ ✦ ✦ ✦ ✦ ✦ ✦ ✦ ✦ ✦ ✦ ✦ ✦ ✦ ✦ ✦

**"All that we see or seem
Is but a dream within a dream."**

— **Edgar Allan Poe** (*American poet and story writer whose stories are among the scariest ever written*)

★ ★ ★ ★ ★ ★ ★ ★ ★ ★ ★ ★ ★ ★ ★ ★ ★ ★ ★ ★

If you want to know more about dreams and dreaming, read:

** *The Dream Game* by Ann Faraday (New York: Harper and Row, 1974).

** *Dream Work* by Jeremy Taylor (New York: Paulist Press, 1983).

** *Creative Dreaming* by Patricia L. Garfield, Ph.D. (New York: Simon and Schuster, 1974).

MYSTERIES OF THE MIND

Have you ever dreamed about something that later came true? Have you ever heard the phone ring and *known* who was on the other end even before answering it? Have you ever had a strange, eerie feeling that a person you've just met is someone you've met before? Have you ever been sure that you were "reading" someone else's mind?

We all experience odd coincidences in our lives. But are they purely accidental? Or is it possible that something really big is going on?

Carl Jung coined the term "synchronicity" to describe coincidences that seem meaningful but have no apparent cause. He believed that these "meaningful coincidences" had their basis in the "collective unconscious" — humankind's shared experiences. Maybe, he suggested, people's unconscious minds were somehow linked with one another.

So far, this is pure speculation. But there does appear to be evidence that the mind perceives the world in ways that the senses do not.

What are the boundaries of the mind? Can these boundaries be transcended? Can the mind go beyond the senses — and beyond time and space? Does the brain give off some sort of physical "energy" that can be detected and decoded?

These are fascinating questions that don't yet have answers. We still don't know enough about the brain and how it works. But it can be fun — and challenging — to speculate.

Parapsychology is a form of research which explores many unexplained phenomena of the mind. These are things that have intrigued and fascinated people for centuries. Even so, some people get upset just thinking about them. They get even more upset when other people claim to have had experiences that aren't easily explained. Parapsychology often arouses people's emotions and prejudices.

Most of the research going on today doesn't try to prove the existence of these phenomena one way or the other. Instead, it explores the possibility that we can learn to develop and use our "mental powers" in our everyday life.

Psychic phenomena may be divided into two categories: mental and physical. Some of these (and we're just scratching the surface) include:

MENTAL	PHYSICAL
ExtraSensory Perception (ESP)	PsychoKinesis (PK)
	Psychic healing
Telepathy	Levitation
Clairvoyance	Out-of-the-body
Precognition	experiences

ESP is something most people have heard of, some people believe in, and other people dismiss as "a bunch of nonsense." "Extrasensory" means "outside the senses" — hearing, sight, touch, taste, and smell. Individuals with ESP can supposedly predict events before they happen, or "know" something that they couldn't have known from the evidence of their senses alone.

ESP is sometimes called the "sixth sense." So is intuition. Perhaps the two are related!

Let's look more closely at some other psychic phenomena. We're also including some simple experiments you can try. When you're through, decide what *you* think!

Telepathy

Telepathy is defined as "mind-to-mind communication between people." Some experts also claim that it occurs between humans and plants, and between humans and animals. In telepathy, information, ideas, and feelings are transmitted directly from one mind to another without the help of the senses.

TELEPATHY EXPERIMENT

What you'll need:

- ► Two people, one to act as the "sender" and the other to act as the "receiver"

- ► A "target object" — a book, a toy, a carrot, a set of keys, or anything else you can think of

- ► A paper bag

- ► Writing paper and a pencil or pen

Before beginning the experiment, the sender puts the target object in the bag without letting the receiver know what it is. Then the sender and the receiver sit in a room with the bag containing the target object.

What to do if you're the sender: Clear your mind of everything except an image of the target object. Concentrate on this image and try to mentally "communicate" it to the receiver. (You may want to close your eyes if that helps you to "focus" more clearly on the object.)

What to do if you're the receiver: Try to "receive" the message from the sender. Close your eyes and imagine the target object — what it looks like, how it would feel if you held it in your hands. Write down or sketch your impressions of or ideas about the target object.

Afterward, compare the receiver's impressions with the target object itself.

If those impressions seem way off, look beyond the obvious. For example, if the object is a carrot and the receiver draws a screwdriver, notice that the two are shaped somewhat the same.

Repeat the experiment, with the sender and the receiver switching roles. Of course you'll have to change the target object.

Clairvoyance

The word "clairvoyance" comes from the French for "clear seeing." If you're looking for something you lost and suddenly have a "hunch" about where it is, you may be using clairvoyance.

Some people seem to have a very strong clairvoyant sense. For example, they can tell when a building is on fire even if they're miles away from it. *Real* clairvoyants often assist the police by locating missing persons or criminals. (We emphasize the word *real* because some clairvoyants are fakes.)

No one knows for sure what clairvoyance is, how it works, or why some people have it while others don't. Maybe *you* have it; here's one way to find out.

CLAIRVOYANCE EXPERIMENT

What you'll need:

◄ Two people, one to act as the "tester" and the other to act as the "subject."

◄ 20 prepared 3×5" cards. The cards should contain the names of 20 related things — for example, musicians or groups, local streets, movie titles, names of athletes, foods. Both the tester and the subject may see the cards before the experiment begins.

◄ Writing paper and a pencil or pen.

The tester and the subject should sit at a table across from each other.

What to do if you're the tester: Shuffle the cards and put them face-down in a pile on the table. Pick up the top card (don't look at it) and place it face-down in front of the subject. After 15 seconds or so, move that card over to the side and place another one in front of the subject. Continue doing this with the rest of the cards in the pile. Whenever you're finished with one card, put it on top of the last one, face-down. (Be sure to keep them in order.)

What to do if you're the subject: Each time the tester puts a card in front of you, concentrate on it. Try to "see" the word or words written on the card. Write down what you think the card says. List your guesses in order on the sheet of paper. (You may want to number them.)

After you've gone through all the cards, turn the pile face-up. Now see how many of the subject's guesses were correct answers, or "hits."

Repeat the experiment, with the tester and the subject switching roles. Or you can do this experiment alone. Shuffle the cards, deal them out to yourself (without looking at them), and write down your guesses.

Precognition

"Precognition means seeing something before it happens." Some people claim to have visions, or "premonitions," of the future.

Many astrologers believe that they can see into the future. Some make "annual predictions;" you may have seen these in the tabloids available at your local supermarket. Tracking these predictions can be fun. Will two gorgeous movie stars get married? Will a political leader make a big mistake? Will someone come up with a new and remarkable invention?

PRECOGNITION EXPERIMENT

Most precognitive experiences seem to occur during dreams, so a good way to find out if you have this talent is by keeping a dream journal for several weeks or months. Then look back at it periodically to see if any of your dreams have come true.

What if you do have a special dream that you're sure is precognitive? How will you be able to prove it later? Your dream journal can serve as one form of backup, but there's another.

Write down when and where the dream occurred and what happened in it. Include as many details as you can remember. Then send this information, along with your name and address, to:

Central Premonitions Registry
Box 402
Times Square Station
New York, NY 10036

Psychokinesis

Telepathy, clairvoyance, and precognition are all *mental* psychic phenomena. Psychokinesis is an especially interesting *physical* phenomenon. It's also known as *telekinesis*.

Basically, psychokinesis is the ability to move objects with your mind. Maybe you've tried it without knowing it. Have you ever been bowling or played pool or horseshoes? Have you concentrated and used "body English" in an attempt to knock the pins down, get the balls in the pockets, or throw "ringers"? (Has it worked?)

You may have seen pictures of people staring at scissors or chairs hanging in mid-air. Are they able to somehow direct their brain waves? Do they have a mysterious mental energy they can call on? No one knows, but it's interesting to think about.

One type of psychokinesis, called "metal bending," is practiced by the famous Israeli psychic Uri Geller. Uri can bend spoons, keys, and other metal objects simply by staring at them!

No one is sure how he does this, but scientists have discovered a clue which may lead toward a solution. They found differences in the molecular structures of two pieces of metal, one of which had been broken by ordinary forces and the other by mental effort.

Interestingly, some metal-benders are children. Maybe it's because they haven't yet told themselves that what they're doing is "impossible!"

Poltergeists

Thanks to Steven Spielberg's movie, a lot of people have at least heard about poltergeists.

The word "poltergeist" means "noisy ghost." Poltergeists have been blamed for falling objects, furniture turned upside-down, objects being thrown across rooms, rapping or knocking sounds, and so on.

The poltergeist phenomena is usually associated with adolescence. Some people believe that it's because many adolescents are calm on the outside and angry on the inside. Their anger builds up and is eventually released as poltergeists.

Matthew Manning is a gifted psychic and author of a book, *The Link*, which tells about his experiences with psychic phenomena.

He reports that he began poltergeist activity at age 11. One night he was working on a school paper when he went into a relaxed state and began writing automatically. When he snapped out of it, he looked at what he had written. It was in a foreign language he had never studied! Not long afterward he took this same approach to drawing and created pictures that look like Picassos.

As Matthew practiced automatic writing and drawing, the poltergeist stuff stopped. Apparently he managed to substitute *productive* activities for the *destructive* activities of his "noisy ghost." This leads to the interesting thought that perhaps psychic energies can be directed.

Many scientists argue that psychic phenomena don't exist, and that any evidence to the contrary must be fake. But if there's anything worse than insisting that a question can have only one answer, it's insisting that it can have *no* answers. That's the same as throwing away the key to a mysterious door that leads ... who knows where?

More and more people are beginning to recognize and accept various forms of psychic phenomena. If even a couple of these strange events are true, then our notion of what it means to be a person must change.

Much of what we call paranormal today may be considered normal in the future. A hundred years from now, people may communicate by sending and receiving mental messages. And they may look back at us and wonder why we couldn't see the obvious!

How can *you* improve *your* psychic abilities? By focusing on developing your *complete* self and paying more attention to the world around you. In fact, two of the goals of psychic development are knowing yourself better and becoming more aware of others. Make those your goals, and your psychic powers may bloom spontaneously and naturally.

If you want to know more about psychic phenomena, read:
** *Seeing with the Mind's Eye* by Mike Samuels, M.D. and Nancy Samuels (New York: Random House, 1975), chapter 16.
** *The Mind Race* by Russell Targ and Keith Harary (New York: Ballantine Books, 1984).

SELECTED BIBLIOGRAPHY

Albrecht, Karl. *Brain Power: Learn to Improve Your Thinking Skills* (Englewood Cliffs, New Jersey: Prentice-Hall, Inc., 1980).

Baddeley, Alan. *Your Memory: A User's Guide* (Middlesex, England: Penguin Books, Ltd., 1983).

Bagley, Sharon, Johnn Carey, and Ray Sawhill. "How the Brain Works," in *Newsweek* (February 7, 1983).

Bloom, Floyd E., Laura Hofstadter, and Arlyne Lazerson. *Brain, Mind and Behavior* (New York: W.H. Freeman and Co., 1985).

Buzan, Tony. *Make the Most of Your Mind* (New York: Linden Press/Simon and Schuster, 1984).

—- *Use Both Sides of Your Brain* (New York: E.P. Dutton, 1983).

Clark, Dr. Barbara. *Growing Up Gifted* (Columbus, Ohio: Charles E. Merrill Publishing Co., 1983).

Cohen, Daniel. *Intelligence: What Is It?* (New York: M. Evans and Company, Inc., 1974).

Corrick, James A. *The Human Brain - Mind and Matter* (New York: Arco Publishing, 1983).

Durden-Smith, Jo, Diane de Simone. *Sex and the Brain* (New York: Warner Books, 1983).

Eberle, Robert. *SCAMPER: Games for Imagination Development* (Buffalo, N.Y.: D.O.K. Publishers, 1971).

Galyean, Beverly - Colleene. "Expanding Human Intelligence," in *The Futurist* (October 1, 1983).

Gardner, Howard. *Frames of Mind: The Theory of Multiple Intelligences* (New York: Basic Books, Inc., 1983).

Hendricks, Gay and Thomas B. Roberts. *The Second Centering Book* (Englewood Cliffs, New Jersey: Prentice-Hall, Inc., 1977).

Hopson, Janet L. "A Magical Memory Tour" in *Psychology Today* (April, 1984).

Kettelkamp, Larry. *Hypnosis: The Wakeful Sleep* (New York: William Morrow & Co., 1975).

McKean Kevin. "In Search of the Unconscious Mind" in *Discover* (February, 1985).

Melmechuk, Theodore. "The Dream Machine" in *Psychology Today* (November, 1983).

Ornstein, Robert and Richard F. Thompson. *The Amazing Brain* (Boston: Houghton-Mifflin Co., 1984).

Osborn, Alex. *Applied Imagination: Principles and Procedures of Creative Problem Solving* (New York: Scribners, 1963).

Restak, Dr. Richard. *The Brain* (Toronto: Bantam Books, 1984).

Russell, Peter. *The Brain Book* (New York: E.P. Dutton, 1979).

Samuels, Dr. Michael and Nancy Samuels. *Seeing with the Mind's Eye* (New York: Random House, 1975).

Signe, Hammer. "Stalking Intelligence: I.Q. Isn't the End of the Line — You Can Be Smarter," in *Science Digest* (June 1985).

Silverstein, Alvin. *Exploring the Brain* (Englewood Cliffs, New Jersey: Prentice-Hall, Inc. 1973).

Sternberg, Robert J. "How Can We Teach Intelligence:" in *Educational Leadership* (September, 1984).

Sternberg, Robert J. "Who's Intelligent?" in *Psychology Today* (April, 1982).

Ward, Brian R. *The Brain and Nervous System* (London: Franklin Watts, 1981).

Willing, Jules Z. *The Lively Mind* (New York: William Morrow & Co., 1982).

N

Nature versus nurture, 43-44
  sex differences and, 56-57
Negative thinking, 75-77
Neocortex, 23
Neurons, 26-27
Newton, Sir Isaac, 36
Nicklaus, Jack, 126
Nierenberg, Gerard I., 94
Nightmares, 124-125
Nonlinear thinking, 65

O

Open-ended thinking, 65
Originality, 65
  creativity and, 102
Ornstein, Robert, 50
Osborn, Alex, 104
Out-of-the-body experiences, 130

P

Parapsychology, 130
Pattern thinking, 51, 65, 74-75
  creativity and, 99
Penfield, Wilde, 83
Personal intelligence, 48
Photographic memory, 84
Picasso, Pablo, 59
Pineal gland, 21
Pituitary gland, 21
Poe, Edgar Allan, 127
Poltergeists, 136
Positive thinking, 75-77
  creativity and, 99
Potential, 60
Precognition, 130, 134-135
Problem solving, 61-63, 65
  creativity and, 97
Processing
  of right hemisphere, 50
  simultaneous, 51
Prodigies, 60
Psychic healing, 130
Psychic phenomena, 130
Psychokinesis, 10, 130, 135-136

R

Rapid Eye Movement (REM), 122-123
RAS. *See* Reticular activating system
R complex, 20
Reasoning, 51
Relationships, 51
Rembrandt van Rijn, 36
Reptilian brain, 20
Rest, brain and, 108-109
Reticular activating system, 22
Rhythm, 51
Ride, Sally, 58
Right-brain functions, 11, 24, 50-53
Rosenzweig, Mark, 16
Rote memory, 88

S

SCAMPER checklist, 104-106
Schiller, Johann, 94
Schulz, Charles, 53
Self-hypnosis, 115-117
Self-image, creativity and, 97
Semantic memory, 84
Sensory memory, 84
Sensory monotony, 115
Sequential thinking, 50, 65
Sex differences in brain, 55-57
Shakespeare, William 79
Shams, Frank, 117
Short-Term memory, 83
Simon, Theodore, 33-34
Simultaneous processing, 51
Sixth sense, 10
Sleep, 119-121
  stages, 120-121
Sleeplearning, 122
Sleeptalking, 121
Sleepwalking, 121
Smell brain, 21
Spatial intelligence, 47, 65
Spatial tasks, 51
Sperry, Roger, 49-50
Spielberg, Steven, 136
Spinal chord, 20
Split-brain surgery, 49
Standardized tests, 40

Stanford-Binet test, 37
Stanley, Julian, 56
Stern, Wilhelm, 34-35
Sternberg, Robert, 30, 45-47
Stevenson, Robert Louis, 126
Stradonitz, Freidrich August Kekule von, 126
Strategic thinking, 77
Stress, 114
Stretching and repetition exercise, 110
Subconscious thinking, 65
Synapse, 27-28
Synchronicity, 129

T

Tacit knowledge, 46
Telekinesis. *See* Psychokinesis
Telepathy, 130-131
Terman, Lewis, 37
Tests, performance on, 40
Thalamus, 21
Theory of Relativity, 52
Thinking skills, 65-79
Thinking on your feet, 77
Tripp, Peter, 119
Truth, logic and, 70

V

Van Der Merwe, Bertha, 119
Verbal, semantic memory, 84
Vertical thinking, 65
Visual thinking, 65, 67-68
Voltaire, 36

W

Washington, George, 36
Wechsler, David, 37
Wechsler Intelligence Scale for Children (WISC and WISC-R), 37-38

Other books for young people by Free Spirit Publishing

Fighting Invisible Tigers
A Student Guide To Life In "The Jungle"

The Gifted Kids Survival Guide
(For Ages 11 - 18)

The Gifted Kids Survival Guide
(For Ages 10 & Under)

Get Off My Brain
A Survival Guide For Lazy Students

For a free copy of our catalog, write:
Free Spirit Publishing Co.
4904 Zenith Ave. So.
Minneapolis, MN 55410